LEADING
WOMEN

Serena Williams

International
Tennis
Superstar

KATE SHOUP

Cavendish
Square

New York

1

Published in 2017 by Cavendish Square Publishing, LLC
243 5th Avenue, Suite 136, New York, NY 10016

Copyright © 2017 by Cavendish Square Publishing, LLC

First Edition

CPSIA Compliance Information: #CS16CSQ

All websites were available and accurate when this book was sent to press.

Library of Congress Cataloging-in-Publication Data

Names: Shoup, Kate, 1972-
Title: Serena Williams : international tennis superstar / Kate Shoup.
Description: New York : Cavendish Square Publishing, [2016] | Series: Leading
Women | Includes bibliographical references and index.
Identifiers: LCCN 2016009005 (print) | LCCN 2016009411 (ebook)
ISBN 9781502620149 (library bound) | ISBN 9781502620156 (ebook)
Subjects: LCSH: Williams, Serena, 1981---Juvenile literature. | Tennis
players--United States--Biography--Juvenile literature. | African American
women tennis players--Biography--Juvenile literature.
Classification: LCC GV994.W55 .S47 2016 (print) | LCC GV994.W55 (ebook)
DDC 796.342092--dc23
LC record available at http://lccn.loc.gov/2016009005

Editorial Director: David McNamara
Editor: Elizabeth Schmermund
Copy Editor: Rebecca Rohan
Art Director: Jeffrey Talbot
Designer: Stephanie Flecha
Production Assistant: Karol Szymczuk
Photo Research: J8 Media

The photographs in this book are used by permission and through the courtesy of:
Richard Shotwell/Invision/AP, cover; Fiona Hamilton/Newspix/Getty Images, 1; Ken
Levine/Allsport/Getty Images, 4, 24; Brad Mangin/Sports Illustrated/Getty Images, 6; Paul Harris/
Online USA/Getty Images, 14; AP Photo/Rick Stevens, 15; AP Photo/Amy Sancetta, 18; Al Bello/
ALLSPORT/Getty Images, 26, 46; AP Photo/Alan Diaz, 32; Scott Barbour/ALLSPORT/Getty
Images, 35; Adam Pretty/AUS /Allsport/Getty Images, 40; Pascal Le Segretain/Getty Images, 43;
Juergen Hasenkopf/REX/Newscom, 47; TOBY MELVILLE/REUTERS/Newscom, 50; SEYLLOU/
AFP/Getty Images, 55; Fairfax Media/Fairfax Media via Getty Images, 58; Al Tielemans/Sports
Illustrated/Getty Images, 64; Bob Martin /Sports Illustrated/Getty Images, 65; Michael Mayhew/
Sportsphoto/Sportsphoto Ltd./Allstar/Newscom, 69; Jimmie48 Photography/Shutterstock.com, 71;
Gary Friedman/Los Angeles Times via Getty Images, 74; JEWEL SAMAD/AFP/Getty Images, 78;
ACE/INFphoto/Newscom, 83; SIMON MAINA/AFP/Getty Images, 87; Theo Wargo/Getty Images
for Sports Illustrated, 91.

Printed in the United States of America

CONTENTS

CHAPTER ONE

The Birth of Two Legends

In 1978, a man named Richard Williams happened to catch a tennis match on television. It was the final match of a women's tournament. A Romanian player named Virginia Ruzici won the match—and to Richard's amazement, claimed a cash prize of forty thousand dollars. That was more than he had earned all year! In her autobiography, *On the Line*, Richard's daughter Serena Williams observed, "It didn't fit with how hard he worked for a living, how hard my mom worked, how hard it was for everyone they knew to get and keep ahead."

This gave Richard an idea: He and his wife Oracene, whom he had met at a bus stop two years earlier, would have two children, and they would play tennis. As he

Serena (*left*) and her sister Venus (*right*) pose for a photo on the tennis court.

later explained, "I was so flabbergasted at the amount of money paid out to professional players." He believed the best thing he could do for his children would be to teach them how to play tennis.

This was, of course, a crazy notion. For one thing, neither Richard nor Oracene, who worked as a nurse, knew how to play tennis. For another, the game was played almost exclusively by rich, white people—and Richard and Oracene were African American. Indeed, by that time, only a handful of African Americans had played tennis at the elite level. One of these professional players was Althea Gibson. In the 1950s, Gibson became the first person of color to win a **Grand Slam tournament**; during the course of her career, she would win eleven in all. (A Grand Slam tournament, also called a major, is one of the more prestigious events on the tennis circuit. There are four Grand Slam tournaments in all: the Australian Open, the French Open, Wimbledon, and the US Open.) The other was Arthur Ashe, who claimed three Grand Slam tournament wins during the 1960s and 1970s.

Nevertheless, this was no pipe dream. Richard Williams was quite serious. He even wrote a seventy-eight-page training plan to prepare for his children's tennis career. "My children will be set apart from the rest of the tennis players," he later wrote in his biography, *Black and White: The Way I See It*. "They won't be set apart because they're African Americans, either. They will be distinguished because they are going to dominate the game."

But first, Richard needed to learn how to play the game himself. He bought a second-hand racquet and 300 used tennis balls. Then he ordered some how-to videos and books and taught himself the game. To improve his footwork, he took dancing lessons. He also took up boxing to improve his coordination.

Next, Richard taught his wife how to play. Oracene was athletic by nature—she had enjoyed volleyball and basketball in her youth—and quickly picked up the fundamentals. After that, Richard taught the game to his three stepdaughters, Yetunde, Isha, and Lyndrea—whom he cared for as he would his own children since their father had died. They would come to enjoy and even excel at tennis (except Yetunde, who, according to Serena, "always said she didn't have an athletic bone in her body."), but they would not reach the heights that Richard Williams had envisioned.

No matter. Richard's next two children—Venus Ebony Starr Williams, born on June 17, 1980, and Serena Jameka Williams, born less than fifteen months later, on September 26, 1981—would achieve all of Richard's wildest dreams.

Moving to Compton

When Venus and Serena Williams were mere infants, their father moved his family from Saginaw, Michigan, to a city known for its high crime rate, Compton, California—not in spite of its violent reputation, but because of it. "My plan was simple: to bring two children out of the ghetto to the forefront of a white-dominated game," Richard wrote.

"I'd always felt that the ghetto makes you tough and strong.' His girls, he believed, "had to learn to be rough, tough, and strong." And so the family settled into their new home at 1117 East Stockton Street.

This type of rough environment was not entirely foreign to Richard. Born in 1942, he had grown up with his four sisters in a three-room shack with a leaky roof in Shreveport, Louisiana. The family had no running water—they used an outhouse in the yard—and no electricity. "Blacks lived in a small area of the city in filthy, old, run-down houses near the railroad tracks, or in dirt road shanties in the woods," Richard later recalled. Although slavery had been abolished in 1865, African Americans like Richard were still second-class citizens. "Too many men got convicted of crimes, real or imaginary, and sent to the State Penitentiary at Angola. Too many more were lynched, burned alive, or beaten to death, their bodies tossed into the nearby Red River," Richard wrote.

Richard's father, R.D., had "a terrible reputation for living off women and having babies all over Shreveport," Richard said. R.D. abandoned Richard and his sisters when the children were young, leaving the hard work of raising five kids to their mother, Julia Mae Williams. Faced with crushing poverty and overwhelming racism, Richard—now the man of the household—turned to crime to support his family. "I became fascinated with stealing at the age of eight," he recalled. Perhaps not surprisingly, Richard often encountered violence. During one childhood fight, he was stabbed in the leg with a railroad spike and an ice pick. During other altercations, Richard was hit over the head with a baseball bat, a bottle, and a flashlight. Many of these confrontations led to arrest.

A Brief History of Tennis

Tennis—from the French word *tenez*, which means "to hold," "to receive," or "to take"—was first played in the twelfth century in northern France. At first, players used the palms of their hands to strike the ball. Later, they wore a glove. By the sixteenth century, the glove had been replaced by a racquet, from the Arabic word *rakhat*, or "palm of the hand." In those days, tennis was played indoors. This form of the game was called *real tennis*.

European royalty loved real tennis. In England, Henry V (1387–1422) was among the first to play. His descendant, Henry VIII (1491–1547), was also passionate about the game. In France, Francis I (1494–1547) was known to play, as was his successor, Henri II (1519–1559).

During the eighteenth and early nineteenth centuries, real tennis died out. In its place came lawn tennis. This form of the game was played outdoors on an hourglass-shaped grass court. Slowly, the game's popularity grew. In 1874, the first lawn tennis court was built in the United States, at the Staten Island Cricket and Baseball Club.

Modern tennis is much like lawn tennis, except the shape and dimensions of the court are different. Rather than an hourglass, the court is shaped like a rectangle. In addition, the net is lower, and the court surface may vary. Some courts are grass, some are asphalt, known as *hard courts*, and some are clay. Finally, modern tennis may be played indoors or outside.

Even so, Compton was a shock to the system. It was, Richard said, "a world of crime and bloodshed." Soon, they "were trapped in the middle of daily gun battles and shootouts." Years later, Serena would remember hearing gunshots from drive-by shootings as she and Venus played tennis. "The shots themselves didn't sound all that terrifying until I learned what they were," she said.

Richard quickly realized that training his girls in Compton would be much harder than he'd thought. His first clue? There were no decent tennis courts in the area. Finally, he found a pair of abandoned courts in a local park. "They had broken glass all over them," he wrote. "They were dirty. There was human waste on them … and anything else you could think of that was filthy or contaminated."

Richard set about cleaning up the courts, only to encounter an even bigger problem: the gangs who claimed that the courts were their turf. He recalled: "In the process of trying to get the gang members to move on I got my teeth knocked out, my nose broken, my jaw broken, and my fingers dislocated. They beat me so badly I could barely walk, but I kept on coming back."

Eventually, Richard established a fragile trust with these gang members, who finally cleared off the courts. "It had taken two years and almost destroyed my body and my spirit, but … none of that mattered," Richard said. "What mattered was the courts were ours." Eventually, as they became accustomed to seeing the girls practice, gang members would even keep a protective eye on the Williams sisters.

"Tennis Dad"

For some reason, tennis attracts fathers (and mothers) who are, in the words of writer Huan Hsu, "obsessive, overbearing, and downright insane." This may explain why many so-called *tennis dads* begin training their children for the sport in their infancy. Take Mike Agassi. When his son Andre was a baby, Mike "designed a special mobile for his crib that consisted of a tennis ball dangling from a wooden Garcia tennis racket." The theory, Mike explained, "was that as Andre grew older, the sight of a tennis ball coming his way would be familiar." Stefano Capriati, whose daughter Jennifer would ascend to the number one ranking after debuting on the pro circuit at the tender age of thirteen, boasted that Jennifer "was doing sit-ups as a baby and had a racket in her hand as soon as she could walk."

Many of these tennis dads are known to behave badly at their children's matches, like Damir Dokic, who coached his daughter, Jelena, to a top-ten ranking during the 2000s. Damir was ejected from three Grand Slam tournaments in one year due to his obnoxious behavior. Jim Pierce, whose daughter Mary won four Grand Slam tournaments between 1995 and 2005, was similarly insufferable. Indeed, Jim was *so* abusive during Mary's matches—toward both Mary and whomever she happened to be playing—the women's tour not only banned him for life, it also changed its rule book to ban abusive players, coaches, and relatives. To this day, this provision is informally known as the "Jim Pierce Rule."

These dads weren't just verbally abusive. Some were even physically abusive. Damir Dokic admitted to hitting his daughter. Jelena later cut ties with her father, after which he threatened to kidnap her. Peter Graf, whose daughter Steffi dominated the women's tour during the 1980s and 1990s, reportedly slapped his daughter "if she missed a shot or failed to perfect a new stroke." (This might explain the nickname given to him by the German press: Papa Merciless.) Jim Pierce would slap his daughter Mary if she lost a match or just had a bad practice.

Some have placed Richard in this same category. Serena has disputed this assessment, however, noting her father's gentle demeanor. Unlike Mike Agassi and Stefano Capriati, Richard waited until his daughters were four years old to introduce them to the game. And at first, he kept things light, just wanting the girls to have fun. He didn't want to force them to play; he wanted them to enjoy it. "I tried to make it fun and I never criticized them, no matter what they did," Richard said.

"Tennis was just something to do, a way for us to be together as a family," Serena recalled. Richard also knew that to make it in tennis, they'd need some innate athletic ability, a passion for

Serena and Richard Williams practice on the courts of Compton.

the game, and the will to succeed—and that each of these characteristics "would take time presenting themselves."

Finally, unlike all those other tennis dads, Richard never put any pressure on his girls. "For my parents, if I never made it as a tennis player, they'd be proud and happy for me, as long as I was doing something that made me proud and happy," Serena wrote. "If I'd just gone to college and played tennis there, that would have been fine. Even if I stopped playing altogether, that would have been fine."

She added, "They only wanted to give us this giant opportunity—after that, it was up to us to make of it what we wanted." Besides, said Richard, "tennis was only a game. That's why they call it 'playing' tennis."

Although Richard has received the lion's share of attention for coaching Venus and Serena in their early years, it was, in fact, a joint effort. Typically, said Serena's half-sister Isha, "Venus would be on my dad's court, Serena would be on my mom's court." Which court was the toughest? According to all the girls, it was Oracene's—no contest. As noted in the *New York Times Magazine*, "Richard liked to play games and goof, but their mother was all business and was matter-of-fact in their criticisms."

Just how did Richard and Oracene—two relative newcomers to the sport—manage to teach their girls so well? "I don't honestly know how that happened," Venus later told a reporter. "I don't know how my parents were able to learn the game so well."

Nevertheless, learn it they did—so well that they would develop not one, but two tennis phenomenons.

Priorities

Serena Williams has said she does not remember her first time holding a racquet. "I just remember playing, all the time. It's like tennis was always there … like breathing."

But Richard and Oracene didn't just train the girls on the tennis courts. Their father, who owned a small security firm, often took the girls to work with him "so they could learn the importance of planning, responsibility, and a strong work ethic, even at their early age." Richard also plastered the fences around their local courts (and, later, the family's front yard) with instructive and inspirational placards. These applied to tennis ("SERENA, YOU MUST LEARN TO USE MORE TOPSPIN ON BALL") and to life ("VENUS, YOU MUST TAKE CONTROL OF YOUR FUTURE"; "SERENA, YOU MUST LEARN TO LISTEN"; "IF YOU FAIL TO PLAN, YOU PLAN TO FAIL").

"He really put a lot of time and effort into this part of our training," Serena recalled, "because he believed it was important. He wanted these messages to resonate, for the visual image of the words to linger in our minds."

Richard and Oracene wanted their daughters to become top-notch tennis players—but they also wanted them to be top-notch human beings. So they made sure to push the girls to work hard in school as well. Richard noted, "During those days, the average education on the women's tour was a junior high school education. I was not going to let that happen to my kids."

Rick Macci, who would later coach both girls, recalled, "I can remember fifty times when [Richard] called off practice because Venus's grades were down." Fortunately, Serena liked school and said that she looked forward to her classes because she loved to learn.

Oracene believed the girls should "lay the foundation for the second act of their lives, even if it sometimes diverts their attention from **forehands** and **backhands**." A big part of this foundation was the girls' faith. At Oracene's insistence, Venus and Serena grew up as Jehovah's Witnesses (although Richard never converted).

"[My dad] and my mom both believed it was important to have religion in our lives. It was a first and foremost deal. That, and a good education," Serena wrote. Even after they became famous, the girls went house to house to spread the word of God.

The Williams sisters were also encouraged to pursue other interests besides tennis. They practiced Tae Kwon Do. They studied ballet and tap. They read and wrote. But two interests were off limits. One was boys. As noted in the *New Yorker*, "Boyfriends were not allowed." The other? Richard also forbade his daughters from playing with dolls. "I had nothing against dolls," he said. "I just didn't want Venus or Serena to believe motherhood was the end goal of their lives when there were so many other goals to be attained."

For Venus and Serena Williams, those other goals would soon be in reach.

CHAPTER TWO

Liftoff

From the time Venus and Serena were very young, their father, Richard, had unwavering confidence in their ability to conquer the tennis world—and he didn't hesitate to say so. As noted in the *New York Times Magazine*, "he billed [Venus and Serena] as celebrities before they were even famous."

Richard's confidence was not misplaced. It quickly became clear that he had been right about the girls' athletic potential. It became even more evident when Venus asked Richard to let her play in some tournaments around Southern California. Richard resisted at first; he believed she wasn't ready. But Venus was persistent. Finally, Richard and Venus made a deal: If Venus could beat Richard in a match, he'd let her play. During the match—which, Serena

Serena Williams triumphantly displays her US Open trophy in 1999.

said, she and her sisters looked forward to "like it was a Wimbledon final"—Venus dismantled Richard's game to beat him fair and square.

Venus—who was tall and strong for her age—dominated the Southern California junior circuit. And Serena—who wouldn't start growing until she was in her mid-teens, and who, as a consequence had to develop a "clever game" —won across the board in what she called "little-kid events."

By virtue of her age, Venus—who Serena often called V—got more attention. Eight-year-old Venus's skill level was described as being on par with "a decent college player." In 1990, when Venus was ten, the *New York Times* published an article about her. In it, former player Jack Kramer described Venus this way: "She's very quick, she has a good sense of tactics, and she has a natural service motion." He went on to say, "For being fourteen, she's pretty good." When someone informed him that Venus had in fact just turned ten, a shocked Kramer replied, "Oh my gosh."

Another former player, Dorothy "Dodo" Cheney, said of young Venus, "Her game had everything. She was fast, she had a spin **serve**, she ran to the net, she had forcing ground strokes, her anticipation was good, and her concentration was excellent." Not surprisingly, Venus also caught the eye of several sponsors, including Wilson, Prince, and Reebok.

"Clearly," Serena wrote in her autobiography, "Venus was the phenom, the prodigy, the rising star. She was the main attraction." And Serena was happy for her! After all, Serena loved Venus. Still, for Serena, it stung that no one seemed to notice *her*, waiting in the wings. Or worse, that they *did* notice her, but immediately dismissed her. "I still remember this one national newspaper article about Venus that suggested I'd never be anything more than a footnote to Venus's career," Serena wrote. "It talked about how in tennis, the younger sibling never amounts to much, and how that would be my fate, too."

In time, Serena would prove them wrong.

Florida Bound

As Venus and Serena progressed in their training, Richard and Oracene realized that the girls needed help from outside coaches. They were also ready to get out of Compton due to the gang-related violence, drug use, and racial tensions.

In 1991, Richard invited Rick Macci, who had coached Jennifer Capriati, to Compton see the girls play. "The only thing I can guarantee you is I won't let you get shot," Richard told Macci, who was understandably nervous about visiting the notoriously violent area. Upon his arrival, Macci went with Richard and the girls to what they called the "Compton Hills Country Club"—in reality, a dilapidated park with two tennis courts that were, in Macci's words, "broken," "chipped up," with broken glass "all over the court." Macci added, "The courts didn't need resurfacing, they needed to be blown up."

At first, watching the girls play, Macci was unimpressed. "I didn't think they were really that good," he recalled. "Technically they were all over the map … You could tell they just didn't have quality instruction." Then Venus played with him, and he saw how hard she fought for the game. She would do anything to get at the ball. "Venus and Serena had a deep down burning desire to fight and compete at this age," Macci said. He was impressed.

Macci said to Richard, "Mr. Williams, it looks like you have the next Michael Jordan on your hands." Richard replied, "'No, Mr. Macci, we've got the next two Michael Jordans.'"

At Macci's urging, Richard and Oracene moved Venus and Serena to West Palm Beach, Florida. Along for the ride were two of the girls' half-sisters (whom Venus and Serena considered to be sisters in full), Isha and Lyndrea. There, Serena and Venus would train at Macci's facility, called Grenelefe. Serena recalled:

Of course, Daddy wasn't prepared to stop coaching us. That wasn't part of the deal. His plan was to work alongside these other coaches and to take advantage of the facilities they offered, and the stronger level of competition, and the new techniques and strategies they might impart. But he would still be our coach. That was never in question.

For Serena, Florida was an adjustment. For one thing, she missed her eldest sister Yetunde. Yetunde, who the girls

called Tunde, had stayed behind in California to pursue
a college degree. For another, where Serena had loved
her school in California, she didn't like her new one in
Florida. Fortunately, the girls were on an accelerated school
schedule, which meant they were on the tennis court by one
o'clock in the afternoon, where they'd stay until about five
or six in the evening.

Not surprisingly, Venus got the lion's share of attention
from the coaching staff at Greenlefe. "These coaches wanted
a chance to work with her and grow their own reputations
on the back of her success, because everyone could see
she'd be a champion," said Serena. "With me, nobody could
really see that just yet. I was still just following in Venus's
footsteps, playing in her shadow."

This cloud did have one silver lining: When Venus was
on one court, working with her new coaches, Serena was on
the next one, working with her dad. "For me, that was one
of the great benefits of being the second string, in terms of
everyone's expectations: I finally had my dad to myself." Yes,
Serena wanted to command the attention of those other
coaches the way Venus did. But, she knew, "I still had to
grow into that priority status."

That's not to say that Serena went completely
unnoticed, however. "The one thing about Serena that stood
out to me was that she was fearless," Macci said later. "She
wasn't afraid to miss. And she hated to lose. She had to
be the first in everything, even if it was getting a drink of
water." Macci added, "I told Richard one of two things was

going to happen: [Serena] will be number one in the world, or she will go to jail."

A Radical Approach

Often, Venus and Serena Williams practiced with the boys—which was, according to Serena, viewed as a "fairly

A young Venus Williams trains at Grenelefe.

radical approach." The girls' game was radical, too. Richard had long believed that women's role in tennis would evolve, and he had trained his daughters to trigger that evolution. "I was out to prove that … powder-puff hitters with lots of spin would no longer dominate tennis," he wrote. "I would introduce a new generation of players: bigger, better, faster, taller."

Perhaps Richard's most radical idea was to keep the girls off of the junior tennis circuit—a grueling series of tournaments all over the world that allows young players to establish their ranking. Serena said, "Daddy just thought we didn't need the pressures of the junior tournament circuit, and he was right about that. He wanted us to have a normal life. He didn't want to be one of those parents pushing and pushing his kids down a path they might not necessarily have chosen for themselves."

The *New York Times Magazine* would call this "Richard's great stroke of genius," explaining that "when the other girls were burning themselves out playing the Young Ladies Lipton Cup or what have you, his girls were hiding, practicing." It is not only physically difficult for young tennis players to play so many tournaments, but it can also be difficult psychologically. Often, younger tennis players feel that they start to dislike the game if they play too many tournaments. Much later, Serena observed. "It turned out to the good … It kept us from burning out on tennis at an early age."

This decision flew in the face of conventional wisdom. Many interpreted it as Richard "thumbing his nose at the tennis establishment," Serena said. "Here was this tall, proud black man from California, who'd never played tennis himself, raising up a real prospect and her kid sister, who might just turn out to be a real prospect as well, and going against the way things were done." But, of course, Richard didn't want to destroy the system—he just wanted to do what was best for his daughters.

Venus Goes Pro

The girls may not have played the junior circuit, but by 1994, shortly after her fourteenth birthday, Venus felt

Venus, age fourteen, playing in her first pro tournament.

she was ready to turn pro. As before, when Venus wanted to start playing the Southern California tennis circuit, Richard disagreed. And as before, Venus prevailed. "Venus can be pretty forceful when she sets her mind to something," Serena wrote.

The tournament was the Bank of the West Classic, in Oakland, California, in November 1994. Serena accompanied her sister, acting as her hitting partner. "Venus really was a star by then," Serena recalled. "She hadn't played a single point as a professional, but everyone knew who she was. She'd been written up in all the tennis magazines and in a lot of major newspapers."

In the first round, Venus drew an American player, Shaun Stafford, ranked number fifty-eight in the world. Venus took her 6-3, 6-4. Next up was Arantxa Sánchez-Vicario, the top **seed** of the tournament, ranked number two in the world. Most people would have been nervous in such a situation, but not Venus.

"She wasn't afraid to go up against a top player like Sánchez-Vicario," Serena recalled. "She just wanted to see what she could do." Venus came out swinging and won the first **set**. In the second set, Venus found herself up 3-0—but then Sánchez-Vicario rallied. Venus would not win another game against the number two player. Serena was "devastated" for Venus. Venus, however, was just happy that she had won her first match and had held her own against a top-seeded player. As far as Venus was concerned, her first match as a pro was a success.

Serena's Turn

Serena was itching to go pro. She was ready, she believed, to follow in her sister's footsteps. In August of 1995, when Venus—who signed a sneaker contract with Reebok that same year for a reported twelve million dollars—played her second pro match (and lost in the first round), Serena lobbied hard to play, too. But Richard—who by then had resumed his role as the girls' primary coach—said no. Serena wasn't ready.

Serena tried a different tactic. She knew the Women's Tennis Association (WTA), which organized the women's tour, planned to up its age eligibility to sixteen starting in 1996. So Serena suggested to Richard that she play at least once in 1995 to establish her eligibility. That way, she'd be grandfathered in under the old age restrictions when the new rules took effect. It was, Richard agreed, a reasonable request.

In the fall of 1995, Richard entered Serena in a professional tournament in Quebec City called the Challenge Bell. It was, said Serena, a "disappointing debut." Unlike Venus, who had drawn a crowd in Oakland, "[Serena] competed on a regulation practice court at a tennis club in suburban Vanier, side-by-side with another qualifying match," noted Robin Finn, a reporter at the match. "There were no spotlights, no introductions, not even any fans." Worse, Serena's opponent, Anne Miller, ranked number 149 in the world, beat Serena 6-1, 6-1. "I felt bad out there because I lost," Serena said after the match. "I didn't play like I meant to play. I played kind of like an amateur."

Scoring Tennis

Tennis uses a unique scoring system. To win a match, a player must win a prescribed number of sets—typically three out of five (men) or two out of three (women). To win a set, a player must win six **games**. However, the player must win by at least two games. In other words, if Player A wins six games and Player B has won five, play must continue. If Player A wins the next game, he or she wins the set. If Player B wins the next game, then the players are tied, and must play a tie breaker. In a tie breaker, the first person to win seven points wins the set—but he or she must win by at least two points.

As for the games themselves, both players start at zero, or **love.** Points then progress to 15, 30, 40, and then game (that is, the game is won). Once again, to win a game, a player must win by at least two points. In other words, if Player A and Player B are tied at 40, Player A must win the next two points to win the game.

If the match is part of a tournament, the winning player moves on to the next round. In the quarterfinal round, eight players remain. In the semifinal round, there are four players. In the final round, there are two players. Whoever wins the final round wins the tournament.

Sometimes, matches involve singles play—that is, one athlete plays against another. Other times, matches involve doubles play—with a team of two athletes playing against another team of two athletes. Mixed doubles means a team is composed of one man and one woman. Often, tournaments feature all three of these types of matches.

"Okay, so I wasn't ready," Serena admitted later. "But I filed the experience away and vowed to learn from it." The biggest lesson? Before, Serena "always expected to win— and I usually did." Now, however, that was not the case. "I could no longer expect to win. I'd have to earn it, fight for it. And I'd have to do it all by myself."

A Taste of Success

Serena Williams would not play a professional match in 1996. Finally, in 1997, ranked 453 in the world, she dipped her toe back into the professional pool. In her first three tournaments back, she lost in the qualifying rounds. Then, finally, came success.

It happened at the Ameritech Cup Chicago, in November 1997. For the first round, Serena—by then ranked number 304—drew the world number 7 player, Mary Pierce ... and *won*. She was similarly successful in the second round, this time ejecting the world number four player, Monica Seles. Ultimately, Serena was stopped by world number five Lindsay Davenport in the semifinals. But still. She had tasted victory—and she liked it. She ended the year ranked ninety-nine.

In 1998, Serena's climb up the rankings continued. That year, Serena also got her first shot at a Grand Slam tournament—four shots, to be exact. At the Australian Open, Serena advanced past the first round, besting Irina Spîrlea, but fell in the second—to her sister Venus. (It was the first match the sisters would play against each other as professionals.) Serena fared better at the remaining Grand Slam tournaments, making it to the third round at Wimbledon and the US Open before falling to Virginia Ruano Pascual and Spîrlea, respectively. And at the French Open, Serena made it to the fourth round, where she was defeated by Arantxa Sánchez-Vicario. She would have more success in mixed doubles, winning the mixed doubles title at Wimbledon and the US Open, with Max Mirnyi. And she and Venus would win doubles titles in Oklahoma and Zurich. At the close of 1998, Serena was ranked number twenty in the world in singles—a meteoric rise.

Venus rose even higher. For the first time, she won a professional tournament—the IGA Tennis Classic in Oklahoma City. She also won the Lipton International Players Championships in Key Biscayne and the Grand Slam Cup in Munich. As for the Grand Slam tournaments, Venus reached the quarterfinals at the Australian Open, French Open, and Wimbledon, and the semifinals at the US Open. On March 30, she broke into the top ten. And by the end of the year, she had had settled in at number five in the world.

In the "Williams Cup," Venus remained ahead. But Serena—who also signed her first sneaker contract in 1998, with Puma—would gain on her soon enough.

Breakout Year

For Serena, 1999 was her breakout year. In February, she won her first pro tournament, the Open Gaz de France, in

Paris—and with it an $80,000 **purse**. (No doubt it occurred to Richard that was *twice* what he'd seen Virginia Ruzici win all those years ago!) Incredibly, Venus also won a tournament—the IGA Super Thrift Classic in Oklahoma City—the very same day.

Serena won her next tournament, too—the Evert Cup, at Indian Wells, California. A Tier 1 tournament, this brought an even bigger payday: $215,000. (In terms of importance in respect to rankings and prize money, Tier 1 tournaments are just a notch below the four Grand Slam tournaments. The tennis circuit also features Tier II, Tier III, and Tier IV events. These tend to offer progressively fewer points and progressively smaller purses.) In August, Serena claimed yet another tournament title—this time the LA Women's Tennis Championships, for another $80,000.

For the first time, Serena played her sister Venus in a tournament final at the 1999 Lipton Championship. Venus won 6-1, 4-6, 6-4.

And in October, she won the Grand Slam Cup in Germany. But the real feather in Serena's cap was winning her first Grand Slam tournament, the US Open, in September, defeating Martina Hingis 6-3, 7-6 to claim a purse of $750,000. For the tennis establishment, this was a wakeup call. All this time, they'd had their eye on Venus—but it was Serena who grabbed the first Grand Slam title in the family! Suddenly, Serena was on their radar. "I think Serena has more clean shots than her sister," Irina Spîrlea said. "She hits the ball harder. She can mix it easier than Venus." Spîrlea added, "[Serena] can be number one."

That's not to say Venus wasn't also on a tear—she was. In all, Venus won six tournaments in 1999. Among these was the Lipton Championships, in which Venus defeated Serena in the finals 6-1, 4-6, 6-4. (A delighted Richard watched the match from the stands, holding a hand-printed sign that read "I TOLD YOU SO.")

Together, the girls were, according to world number one Martina Hingis, "the strongest opponents on tour." Of the pair, Spîrlea observed, "They have something the others don't have." At the close of the year, both Williams sisters had landed in the top five in the rankings—Serena at number four and Venus at number three.

The Williams sisters—both of them—had arrived.

CHAPTER THREE

Bumps in the Road

For the most part, 1999 was a wonderful year for Serena. At last, she'd found success on the tennis court and was receiving the attention she believed she deserved. But one event cast a pall that year: her parents' announcement that they were divorcing.

"What happened to us?" Richard wrote of his divorce. "Well, the power of money and success drives professional sports in America, and if you are not careful, you can easily succumb to it." He continued, "Great success brought with it problems we had never imagined, some of which we were unable to face wisely." Some outlets reported that Richard had beaten Oracene badly enough to break a few ribs—a report that Oracene confirmed but Richard denied.

2001 was a difficult year for Serena Williams due to professional losses and personal struggles.

Still, he wrote, "Oracene is an amazing force for good in this family, and she remains one of the best women I have ever known in my life."

"It threw me," Serena said of the divorce. But, she noted, she and Venus were pretty much adults by then. "A divorce wasn't going to change our lives all that much," she said. Serena and Venus realized that if her parents weren't happy together, then it would be better for both of them if they divorced. Serena continued, "I loved them dearly. We all did. That wasn't about to change. And we all knew they loved us right back. That wasn't going to change, either."

A Plateau

Serena started the 2000 tennis season with high expectations. However, she would soon be disappointed.

First, the good news. Serena defended her title at the LA Women's Championships and picked up two other tournament wins: the Faber Grand Prix in Germany and the Toyota Princess Cup in Japan. But she failed to defend her titles in Paris, Indian Wells, and worst of all, the US Open, where she lost in the quarterfinals. She did slightly better at Wimbledon, falling in the semifinals to Venus (who would go on to win the tournament—her first Grand Slam title), but she lost in the fourth round at the Australian Open. And, due to an injury, she missed the French Open altogether. Still, Serena ended the year ranked number six in the world, falling just two spots from the year prior. Venus remained at number three.

The 2001 season was similarly disappointing. Although Serena won three tournaments, she suffered only heartbreak at the Grand Slam events. Martina Hingis bounced her from the Australian Open in the quarterfinals. Jennifer Capriati bested her in the quarterfinals at the French Open and again at Wimbledon. (Speaking of Wimbledon, Venus successfully defended her title there.) And in the finals of the US Open, Serena lost to Venus. Once again, Serena finished the year sixth in the standings. And once again, Venus was ranked third.

Trouble at Indian Wells

For Serena, the year 2001 was disappointing for yet another reason. That year, at Indian Wells, Serena, Venus, and Richard found themselves facing a jeering, angry, downright racist crowd.

Why the **vitriol**? Throughout the tournament, both Serena and Venus played well. Both women advanced to the semifinal round, where they would face each other. But during her quarterfinal bout, Venus hurt her knee.

Venus had hoped to recover before her match with Serena. But when she woke up that morning, she knew it was a no-go. Her knee was too sore. She hated to disappoint the tournament organizers, television partners, and fans, but she had no choice. She would have to withdraw, which meant Serena would automatically advance to the finals. As Richard observed, "If Venus played hurt, she risked permanent injury and, potentially, the end of her career." According to Serena, "She didn't want to withdraw, but she believed she had no choice." Venus informed tournament officials that she could not play the match. But instead of canceling the match right away, the officials told her to hold off on making her final decision. There was a lot riding on the match. As Richard noted, "Thousands of people had paid good money to see Venus and Serena play, and hundreds of tournament organizers had worked for weeks or months and had millions of dollars at stake." So they stalled.

And stalled.

And stalled.

Finally, five minutes before the match was set to start— long after the crowd had filed in and found their seats—a tournament spokesperson announced that the match had been cancelled. "Well, the place went nuts—and not in a good way," Serena recalled. "The fans were angry." Serena understood why they were upset. "I would have been mad, too, if I'd paid my money and gone to all the hustle and hassle of getting to the stadium." But, she continued, "what I couldn't understand was why the anger was directed at us."

Nevertheless, the late announcement made people in the crowd think that the Williams sisters had been inconsiderate and didn't care about their fans. Suddenly, Richard observed, "we, and especially me, were accused of everything from fixing the match to manipulating the rankings." (Indeed, accusations of match fixing would dog the family for years—an allegation Serena found "absurd" and "enraging.") But, they assumed, it all would blow over.

Unfortunately, it didn't.

When Serena stepped on the court on the day of the final, she was met with a chorus of boos. "It wasn't just a scattered bunch of boos," Serena recalled. "It was like the whole crowd got together and decided to boo all at once." But things didn't stop there. The crowd yelled racial epithets at Serena on the court, and at Venus and Richard in the stands. "I was devastated," Richard recalled. "How could the same racial issues I confronted in 1950 reach across time and imperil my daughters?" He went on, "Blacks have long been accustomed to being second-class citizens. Here was proof that race still played a role in sports." As for Serena, she wanted to cry … but she didn't. "I didn't want to give these people the satisfaction, or let them know they could get to me." She gathered her strength, and she played.

Not surprisingly, Serena got off to a rocky start, losing the first set to her opponent, Kim Clijsters, 4-6. No doubt, Serena was rattled. It didn't help that the crowd applauded each time she made a mistake and jeered each time she won a point. But in the second set, Serena turned things around, winning 6-4. And in the third, she broke Clijsters's serve twice to win 6-2. "I don't know how I did it," she said later. "But what mattered to me most of all at just that moment was that it was over." She continued, "It wasn't about winning. It was about powering through."

Kim Clijsters, actress Holly Hunter, and Serena Williams following the final at Indian Wells in 2001.

After the match, Serena showed true courage. "First and foremost," she said during the post-match interview, "I'd like to thank my God, Jehovah, because you guys were a little tough on me today. I'd like to thank my dad, my family, my sisters, and the sponsors. And I'd like to thank Kim for providing such a wonderful final." Then—and it was here that Serena showed real grace—she said, "I'd like to thank everyone who supported me, and if you didn't, I love you guys anyway." And with that, she held her head high, waved to the crowd, and left the court.

Clearly, there had been a racist element to these attacks. "Here was the truth of that day," Richard noted. "A doctor confirmed Venus's injury and instructed her not to play. The decision was met with suspicion and distrust because we were not white." He said, "My daughters were treated without an ounce of dignity or respect. They were treated like criminals."

Serena agreed. "If it had been twenty years earlier and Chris Evert had to make a late scratch in a semifinal against her sister Jeanne, nobody would have booed Jeanne the next day."

It would be years before Serena, heartbroken by what happened at Indian Wells, would return there. Even though the tournament had become a mandatory event, meaning players could be fined or suspended if they failed to attend, she boycotted it for more than a decade.

Heartbreak

Serena suffered one more heartbreak in 2001—this one of a more personal variety. Earlier that year, she'd fallen in love. The object of her affections? Serena declined to say—she referred to him in her autobiography simply as *So-and-So*—but sources indicate he was an NFL player. "I thought I was in love," Serena said later.

Out of nowhere, in the fall of that year, So-and-So just … disappeared.

"I didn't know what to do," Serena recalled. "This was my first serious relationship. I had no road map to follow, to tell me how to respond when someone you thought you loved wouldn't even return your phone calls." She continued, "This guy tore my heart in half. Then he ripped up those pieces and stepped on them and backed his car up

Forgiveness

Serena swore neither she nor Venus would ever return to Indian Wells. It was, for her, a point of pride. But in 2015, Serena changed her mind. Admittedly, she was nervous. "What if I walked onto the court and the entire crowd booed me?" she wrote in *Time* magazine. "The nightmare would start all over." But, she continued, "I play for the love of the game. And it is with that love in mind, and a new understanding of the true meaning of forgiveness"— which Serena had developed while reading the autobiography of one of her idols, Nelson Mandela, whom she had met in Africa in 2008—"that I will proudly return to Indian Wells in 2015." She added, "Indian Wells was a pivotal moment of my story, and I am part of the tournament's story as well. Together we have a chance to write a different ending."

Serena was not disappointed. During her first match of the tournament, she received a standing ovation. In an ironic turn, Serena herself was forced to withdraw from the semifinal match due to an injured knee, as her sister had done in 2001. Although the announcement of her decision was met with a few scattered boos, by and large, the crowd showed their appreciation and admiration for a player who had endured—and achieved—so much. They shared the sentiments of the stadium announcer: "You belong here, we love you, and welcome back to Indian Wells!"

over them." Serena was heartbroken. But she knew what to do. "Tennis would be my salvation."

And it was.

The Serena Slam

In late 2001, after her breakup, Serena went to Germany to play in a tournament—and, despite her disappointing year to that point, she won. It was incredibly satisfying. "I wanted So-and-So to regret how he treated me," she said. "I wanted him to see me everywhere, doing well. That became my focus. Nothing was more important." Looking back, Serena would concede that she was "playing for all the wrong reasons." But, she thought, "what did I care, if all the wrong reasons ended up taking me to the same place as all the right ones?"

Unfortunately, Serena was forced to sit out of the 2002 Australian Open due to an ankle injury. But after extensive rehab, she was back soon enough. She won her very next tournament, the State Farm Women's Tennis Classic in Scottsdale, Arizona, defeating Jennifer Capriati in the final. Next up was the Miami Open, where Serena dismantled world number three Martina Hingis in the quarterfinal, world number two Venus in the semifinal (just the second time Serena had beaten her sister in tournament play), and world number one Capriati in the final. She was slightly less successful in her next two tournaments, losing in the quarterfinals in Charleston and the finals at the German Open. But she won the Italian Open, her first clay-court title. In doing so, Serena rose to a career-high third in the rankings.

Serena Williams celebrates her first French Open title in 2002.

But Serena was just getting started. At the 2002 French Open, one of the four Grand Slam tournaments, Serena defeated Venus in the final to claim her second career major. This put her at number two in the world—second only to her sister, who had recently risen to number one for the very first time in her career. For Serena, this was a momentous occasion. "It was such a long time coming," she said. "Daddy was always telling reporters and anyone else who'd listen that someday we'd be number one and number two in the world." She continued, "and I remember feeling so happy for him when it finally played out just as he'd foretold."

Serena wasn't finished. At Wimbledon, Serena again defeated Venus in the final—without losing a single set. With this last victory, Serena dethroned her sister in the rankings. At last, *she* was the number one player in the world. Her performance at the US Open proved that this was no fluke; Serena again conquered Venus in the finals, winning straight sets to claim the title. And before the year was out, Serena would win two more titles—in Tokyo, Japan, and Leipzig, Germany. By the end of 2002, Serena had compiled a win-loss record of 56-5, claimed eight singles titles, and finished the year ranked number one in the world.

Serena charged out of the gate in 2003 to win the Australian Open—her fourth Grand Slam tournament in a row. With this victory, Serena became only the sixth woman in the **Open Era** to complete a **career Grand Slam** and the fifth woman to hold all four Grand Slam titles

With her victory at the Australian Open in 2003, Serena Williams completed her first Serena Slam.

simultaneously. (The Open Era began in 1968. Starting that year, professional players were allowed to compete in Grand Slam tournaments. Before that, only amateurs were permitted.) The press would dub this feat the *Serena Slam*. (Incredibly, Serena would complete a second Serena Slam in 2014–2015.) Serena called it something else: her *So-and-So Slam*.

Serena captured two more singles titles—at the Open Gaz de France and the Sony Ericsson Open—before her next major, the French Open. There, despite being the top seed, Serena felt the sting of defeat—this at the hands of Justine Henin, in the semifinals. Wimbledon, however, told a different tale. Serena defeated Henin in the semifinals and Venus in the finals for her second consecutive Wimbledon title.

No doubt, with all this success, So-and-So took notice. But by then, Serena didn't care anymore. She'd fulfilled her destiny. "Four Grand Slam tournament titles in a row," she said. "Each on the back of an unfortunate piece of rejection and dejection—and each a reminder that it's in the picking ourselves up and dusting ourselves off and pushing ourselves forward that we find our will, our drive, our purpose."

A Devastating Loss

Serena maintained her position as world number one for fifty-seven weeks. But shortly after Wimbledon, she suffered—of all things—a dancing injury. While at a club in Los Angeles, Serena, dancing in heels, made a wrong move and hurt her knee—an injury that would require surgery to correct. Instead of playing the US Open, Serena found herself laid up, with little to do but rehabilitate her knee … and watch her ranking slide. Unable to compete for the rest of the year, she would finish it ranked number three in the world.

This was bad—but things were about to get much, much worse.

On September 14, 2003, Serena's beloved big sister, Yetunde was murdered in Compton—shot in the head by a gang member as she rode in a car with her boyfriend, Rolland Wormley. Just thirty-one years of age, Yetunde, who had been a nurse and successful businesswoman, left three young children behind.

"These guys just started opening fire," Wormley—who had a criminal record—told the L.A. Times after the shooting. "We were just innocent passersby." Later, Richard would discover that the shooting had been an accident. The *real* target had been Wormley.

Serena was devastated. "Gone?" she wrote in her autobiography. "There was just no way. It was too crazy. Too impossible. Too sad." She continued, "The next days and weeks were a blur." She turned to her family and friends for support. Even So-and-So resurfaced to offer a shoulder, as a friend.

Tennis was now the last thing on Serena's mind.

CHAPTER FOUR

Back to the Top ... Twice!

After the death of her sister, Serena was, as she said, "adrift for a while." When her knee finally healed, she returned to tennis—but her heart still wasn't in it.

Given her state of mind, it was no surprise to Serena that she was off her game. Yes, she won a title in Miami in April of 2004, her first tournament back, and another in Beijing, in November. And yes, she made it to the finals at Wimbledon, where she lost to Maria Sharapova in straight sets. But overall, Serena's 2004 season was far from stellar. She even dropped out of the top ten for the first time in ages. "My drive, my sense of mission and purpose, my desire

Serena celebrates a winning point at Wimbledon in 2005.

to be the best in the world … all these things had fallen away without me realizing it, and it wasn't clear if I'd ever get them back," she said later.

At the start of 2005, it appeared things were looking up. Serena won the Australian Open for the second time. But then, Serena said, "I lapsed into serious downhill mode." Not only did she fail to win another tournament all year, she never even made it to the finals. What was going on? Serena just couldn't bring herself to care about tennis. In fact, she had even come to resent the game. "I was slipping into a depression," she explained later. She described her condition as "an aching sadness, an allover weariness, a sudden disinterest in the world around me—in tennis, above all."

Finally, in January 2006, at the Australian Open, Serena broke down. Halfway through her third-round match, she said, "All I could think was that I so didn't want to be out there, at just that moment. On the court. In Melbourne. Fighting for points I didn't really care about." And she started crying during her match, right on the court. To her relief, no one saw it. Her tears were masked by her sweat. But "it was such a low, despairing, *desperate* moment for me," she said later. She lost the match in straight sets, but she hardly cared. "I still remember walking to the players' locker room after the match feeling so completely lost and beaten and confused."

After the match, Serena flew home. It would be months before she picked up her racquet again.

Life Support

Toward the end of 2005, Serena—having realized she was seriously depressed—began seeing a therapist. At first it was once a week. Then it was every few days. Finally, after her breakdown in Australia, she went every day. Slowly, with the help of her therapist and her family and friends, Serena returned to life—and to tennis.

One day, walking near her home, Serena encountered a young African-American girl. "You're Serena Williams!" the girl said, her face lit up with a smile. The two chatted, and then the girl—who had commented on Serena's absence from the tour—said something that stuck with Serena: "I hope you come back because you're still a great player. I just know you'll come back and be better than ever."

This moved Serena—and it also got her to thinking: Maybe that little girl was right. Maybe Serena *could* come back and be better than ever! Inspired, Serena went home and watched some footage of past matches. "Right away," she said, "it reminded me how much I used to enjoy winning." She also watched some footage of other players. "I can beat those girls," she thought. "In my sleep, I can beat those girls." The very next day, Serena signed up for a tournament in Cincinnati, in July. It would be her first tournament in six months.

The Comeback Kid

Serena was in terrible physical condition. But she knew that the longer she stayed away from tennis, the harder it would be to come back. So even though her fitness was lacking, and she'd put on a few pounds, and she hadn't picked up a racquet for months, she returned to the game. "I figured I could play myself back into form," she said. All this is to say that Serena—who had fallen to number 139 in the world—wasn't expecting much of herself at that tournament in Cincinnati.

Incredibly, despite these disadvantages, Serena advanced to the semifinals in Cincinnati, where she finally lost to Vera Zvonareva. Of her run in the tournament, Serena said, "I actually surprised myself—I surprised a lot of people, I think." Serena had a similar run at her next tournament, the JP Morgan Chase Open, in Los Angeles. Once again, Serena advanced to the semifinals, this time losing to Jelena Janković.

Next up was the US Open, looming large over Serena's schedule. Due to her ranking, now number ninety-one in the world, Serena would—for the first time in her career—have to qualify for the tournament. She did so handily, but fell in the fourth round to Amelie Mauresmo of France. Still, Serena had reason to celebrate: she had won her middle set against Mauresmo 6-0. "That's always a powerful calling card, when you can break a top player three times in a single set." She continued, "When you're coming back from nowhere at all, you take your accomplishments where you can find them."

It was true: Serena wasn't playing at her top form … *yet*.

An Inspiring Trip

In November 2006, Serena took a life-changing journey to West Africa—Ghana and Senegal to be exact—to tour the region, to visit some schools, to give some tennis clinics, and, in conjunction with the United Nations Children's Fund (UNICEF), to distribute vaccinations, medicine, and bed nets to help combat malaria, a disease spread by mosquitos.

It was this last task, working with UNICEF, that really moved Serena. "It was impossible to visit these remote, impoverished villages and not be moved by the plight of the people there," she said. "It was such a gratifying feeling to know we were helping people who couldn't really help themselves."

Serena, during her 2006 visit to West Africa.

Why West Africa? She wasn't sure why, but Serena had always believed that like many Africans who had been sold into slavery and shipped to North America, her ancestors had hailed from that area. With that in mind, Serena also visited several so-called slave castles. These imposing structures, situated on the coast, had served as way stations for the slave trade. Africans who were captured in the continent's interior were brought to these slave castles. "If they survived the weeks-long warehousing and starvation that followed," Serena wrote, "they were packed into waiting ships and sent off to North America." Many would die on the journey of disease. Those who survived faced a lifetime of servitude in brutal and dehumanizing conditions. "Literally, only the strong survived," she said. "You had to be pretty strong just to make it across the ocean."

Serena could not help but be moved by these slave castles. "I didn't think I would cry," she said. "But of course I cried." She continued, "How could you help but realize that one of your ancestors—someone with your blood!— survived these tortuous conditions so that you could stand in his or her place?"

But she felt something else, too: pride. "I came away thinking I was part of the strongest race in human history," she said. "After all, if we weren't strong, I wouldn't be here." She realized, "There's nothing that can break me. On the court. Off the court. Anywhere." It was, she said, "an incredibly empowering experience, and an equally empowering realization."

An Incredible Upset

Serena arrived in Melbourne in January 2007 for the Australian Open, having not won a tournament since 2005. She was, in her own words, still "seriously out of shape and nowhere in the rankings." She continued, "The general consensus was I was a big fat cow."

She was washed up, people said. Her best days on the court were behind her. Winning the championship was a pipe dream. "So many people were counting me out, the same way they had when I first came up," Serena said. But she hung tough. She stayed focused. "I wasn't about to let these people get to me," she said. She drew strength from that trip to West Africa and her realization about her strength and the strength of her ancestors. "I can do anything," she thought. "There will be no stopping me. Nothing can break me."

Still, the task before Serena was daunting. To win the title, she would have to defeat six well-ranked players—a feat that had never before been achieved. First up was Mara Santangelo. Serena beat her in straight sets. Next came Anne Kremer. She, too, fell to Serena. After that, Serena picked off Nadia Petrova, Jelena Janković, Shahar Peer, and Nicole Vaidišová. These were "Good players. Strong players. Players who certainly didn't expect an overweight, out-of-shape, has-been champion like me to give them a game." To everyone's astonishment, Serena—the "fat cow"—had made it to the finals. She faced Maria Sharapova.

"I would not be denied," Serena said—and indeed, she wasn't. She gave Maria Sharapova a positive shellacking, beating her 6-1, 6-2. "I would prove everyone wrong, and in doing so I would prove something to myself," she wrote. "That I was back where I belonged, playing tennis at a high level, fighting for Grand Slam tournament titles, making my mark." In a touching tribute, Serena dedicated her victory to her sister Yetunde.

A triumphant Serena Williams after her 2007 Australian Open win.

Serena's win in Melbourne would prove to be the high point of 2007. She would claim just one other title—in Miami. But she didn't mind. By the end of the year, she had clawed her way back into the top ten. But more importantly, she was "back in the discussion. Back in the game."

Back On Top

The next year, 2008, Serena would not repeat her Australian Open win; she was bounced from the quarterfinals by Jelena Janković. But she won her next three tournaments, in Bangalore, Miami, and Charleston. "I was Serena Williams. Again. At last. And I would not be denied."

Well, she would be denied—at least sometimes. Like when she was upset in the third round at the French Open. And when Venus defeated her in the finals at Wimbledon. But each time Serena fell, she simply picked herself up and dusted herself off.

By the time the US Open rolled around, Serena was ready. This time, she faced Venus in the quarterfinals—and won. Suddenly, it became doubly important that Serena take the title. "Venus had been playing so well that I know she'd have gone on to win the championship if I hadn't knocked her from contention, so now I had to win," she said. There was one more incentive, however: by winning the tournament, Serena would again claim the number-one ranking.

Incredibly, Serena did just that, defeating Dinara Safina in the semifinals and Jelena Janković in the finals. Once again, for the first time since 2003—and just two years after bottoming out at number 139—Serena was the best female tennis player in the world.

Another Setback

By the end of 2008, Serena would drop one spot to number two. But she would quickly reclaim the top spot, winning both the Australian Open and Wimbledon in 2009. Then an incident in 2010 stopped her short.

It was unfortunate, because Serena had been on a tear. Once again, she had won the Australian Open. And at Wimbledon, she absolutely dominated the field. Indeed, Serena did not lose a single set in the tournament. But in July, while at a restaurant, Serena stepped on broken glass and cut her foot—an injury that would sideline her for the remainder of the year. (Still, despite having played just six tournaments in 2010, she ended the year ranked number four.)

One might think that a cut on the foot would be a minor matter. Not so for Serena. Due to the severity of the cut, her injury required multiple surgeries. Afterward, Serena was forced to wear a cast on her foot for ten weeks, followed by another ten weeks in an orthopedic boot. Then things took an even scarier turn: In February 2011, Serena experienced shortness of breath and severe swelling in her leg. Doctors quickly discovered that she had developed a pulmonary embolism (PE), or a blockage of the lung's main artery. This was serious; severe cases of PE can cause death.

Fortunately, doctors were able to treat the PE by injecting blood thinners. But this treatment resulted in yet another problem: a hematoma in Serena's abdomen, which required surgery to remove. "This has been extremely hard, scary, and disappointing," Serena told reporters.

Tennis's Original Sister Act

Long before Venus and Serena, there was another pair of African-American sisters in the tennis world: Roumania and Margaret Peters, who played in the American Tennis Association from 1938 to 1953.

Often compared to the famous Negro Leagues in baseball, the American Tennis Association (ATA) was formed in 1916 by a group of prominent African-American men in response to the whites-only United States Lawn Tennis Association (USLTA), later called the United States Tennis Association (USTA), which remains the sport's governing body in the United States. Until the desegregation of the USLTA in the 1950s, the ATA was the governing body for African-American tennis in the United States.

During their career, the Peters sisters won fourteen ATA doubles titles. In addition, Roumania won two singles titles, in 1944 and 1946. In the second of these, she defeated Althea Gibson, who would go on to win Wimbledon and the United States National Championships (later called the US Open) during the 1950s.

Roumania died in 2003, at the age of eighty-five. Her sister Margaret died one year later, at the age of eighty-nine. "I know they loved watching Venus and Serena play," Roumania's daughter, Frances Walker Weekes, later told the *New York Times*.

Coming Back ... Again

Finally, in June 2011—nearly one year after she cut her foot—Serena returned to tournament play. Things were slow going—at least at first. Serena lost in the second round of the Aegon International in the United Kingdom and the round of sixteen at Wimbledon. Her ranking was similarly disappointing, bottoming out at 169. But Serena didn't worry. After all, she'd fallen in the rankings before and clawed her way back up; she knew what it took to do it again. She won her next two tournaments, at Stanford and in Toronto. And she made it to the US Open finals, although she lost to Australian Samantha Stosur. By the end of the year, she was ranked twelfth in the world.

Her ascent continued in 2012. In April, she claimed the Family Circle Cup in Charleston. Then she won the Mutua Madrid Open in May. There was one bump in the road—Virginie Razzano defeated Serena in the first round of the French Open. But Serena bounced back at Wimbledon, claiming her fifth title, thanks in part to the 102 aces she delivered throughout the course of the tournament. After that, Serena won three of her four remaining tournaments of the year, including the US Open and, for the first time in singles play, the London Olympics. There, she trounced Maria Sharapova in the gold-medal match. (Serena and Venus had won gold in doubles play in 2008—a feat they repeated in 2012.) With this victory, Serena completed a career Golden

Slam—winning all four Grand Slam tournaments plus the Olympic gold medal. Once again, Serena broke into the top ten, finishing the year at number three.

Finally, in 2013, Serena Williams would again reach number one. To achieve this, she reached thirteen finals and won eleven titles—including the French Open and the US Open. With this last victory, Serena—at thirty-two years of age—became the oldest player to win the US Open in the Open Era. It also propelled her past the $50 million mark in prize money.

Serena remained at number one for all of 2014, despite losing the Australian Open, the French Open, and Wimbledon. She returned to form at the US Open, winning the title. This would mark the first win of a second Serena Slam, which Serena would complete in 2015 after winning the Australian Open, the French Open, and Wimbledon. Serena remains at the number one spot at the time of this writing.

For the second time in her career, Serena had fallen in the rankings. And for the second time, she came back, better than ever!

CHAPTER FIVE

Serena's Legacy

Serena Williams achieved all that she ever dreamed of in tennis—and more. She has been ranked number one on six different occasions, and remains at that position at the time of this writing. Serena's win at Wimbledon in 2015 marked her twenty-first Grand Slam tournament victory in singles play, the most of any woman in the Open Era save one: Steffi Graf, who during her illustrious career won twenty-two. Serena has also claimed thirteen Grand Slam women's doubles titles (many with her sister Venus) and two Grand Slam mixed doubles titles, for a whopping thirty-six major titles in all. All this helps to explain why, during the course of her career, Serena has won more prize money than any other female player. Her $74,083,421 career total (as of

A victorious Serena Williams following her 2015 Wimbledon win

December 2015) is more than double that of the next player down, Maria Sharapova. (Venus is third on the list, with career earnings of $32,608,015.) In fact, it's more than any female athlete in any sport has won.

The consensus among players past and present is that Serena is the greatest ever to play the game. "Nobody has had a game like hers," said tennis legend Chris Evert. "Nobody has had the power and the shots and the serve and the complete package that she has, so she's the best tennis player." Evert has described Serena as, "a phenomenon that once every hundred years comes around." Despite being married to Steffi Graf, men's star Andre Agassi concurs. Regardless of whether Serena surpasses his wife's record of twenty-two wins, he said, "She's arguably the greatest ever." John McEnroe, too, described Serena as "the greatest player, I think, that ever lived."

Some, like author Ian Crouch, say she's the greatest American athlete of her generation, bar none. "When I say the greatest athlete in a generation," Crouch said, "I mean

the greatest in any sport"—among both men and women. After all, as noted by Matt Schiavenza

Serena Williams flanked by two other tennis legends: Martina Navratilova and Chris Evert.

in the *Atlantic*, no other athlete—not LeBron James, not Tiger Woods—has "matched Williams' combination of dominance and longevity."

It is perhaps her longevity that is most impressive about Serena. Schiavenza observed, "The arc of a typical professional tennis player tends to resemble that of a pop star: ascendant at seventeen, dominant at twenty-one, washed up and finished by thirty." And yet, Serena has played well into her thirties. At the time of this writing, she is thirty-four years of age. (Venus, too, has continued to play, although health issues have slowed her down.) Schiavenza added, "Serena, unlike the others, has forgotten to go into decline."

In 2015, Brad Gilbert, a former player who is now a top coach, told *Vogue*, "It is unbelievable what Serena is doing right now. She won her first major at seventeen, and now she's winning at the age of thirty-three? That's a range of sixteen years." Gilbert added, "Whether for men or women, that kind of longevity in tennis is unheard-of."

Incredibly, Serena's not finished yet—and she has said that she never wants to stop. As noted by Schiavenza, "We're watching one whose greatest accomplishments, improbably, may be yet to come."

Tennis Revolutionary

According to journalist J.A. Allen, "When historians of the future look back on the women's tennis game, they will certainly point to one event that changed the course of the

63

game more significantly than any other." That event? The arrival of the Williams sisters. Venus and Serena have done more than succeed at tennis. They have revolutionized the women's game.

"Before them," recalled African-American standout James Blake, women could "dominate just with ... skill and finesse." A contributor at *tennishead* magazine put it this way: "Women's tennis once resembled a chess-like battle of tactical wit, as players entertained the masses with displays of artistry, finesse, and flair. Players would slice and dice, chip and charge, serve and **volley,** in an effort to utilize every shot in the book to outmaneuver an opponent."

Venus and Serena changed all that. They "have redefined the sport around power," said the *New York Times.* As a result, female players are now "stronger, bigger, faster, better trained and pushed above all by the example of the Williams sisters." Other players agree. As noted by Belgian champion Kim Klijsters, "Venus and Serena raised the bar for everyone." And tennis legend Billie Jean King has said,

"My lord, what I would give to hit one ball like them."

Their primary weapon? The serve. According to

Serena Williams, age thirty-three, competes at the 2015 French Open.

Serena Williams prepares to deliver her famous powerful serve.

tennishead magazine, "While the serve was once used as a means of starting the point, Venus and Serena were ending points with it." Venus has clocked the second-fastest serve ever on the women's tour, at 129 miles per hour. But Serena's serve is even more feared. J.A. Allen said, "Serena's serve is not only powerful, but also consistent, effortless and precise. It has been called the best serve ever in the history of women's tennis." The sisters' **groundstrokes** are similarly powerful. In 2014, Serena's forehand was ranked number one on the tour by more than two dozen leading coaches, players, and analysts. And her two-handed backhand was ranked number two.

As noted by J.A. Allen, "The power game, as introduced by the Williams sisters over a decade ago, has raised the bar in women's tennis." Because of Venus and Serena, "Women playing today are stronger, more fit, and more able to blast winners from the back of the court."

Combatting Sexism

"Women can do anything," Richard Williams wrote in his autobiography. "I taught my girls that. I never gave them any sense that they were less than boys, that they weren't as good, or that they were inferior or subservient to anyone in any way." He noted, "I wanted to teach **Venus** and Serena that being a woman wasn't a disadvantage, it was an advantage." Unfortunately, not everyone holds this enlightened view. Because of their size, strength, and

Types of Tennis Shots

In tennis, there are several different types of shots. There's the serve, which is the shot that puts the point in play. The player stands at the baseline, tosses the ball into the air, and brings the racquet up overhead to make contact with the ball. A forehand is a typical tennis shot—the player swings the racquet along the side of his or her body palm first. With a backhand, the player swings the racquet across his or her body, with the back of the hand preceding the palm. Both the forehand and backhand are typically groundstrokes—that is, they bounce off the ground before being struck by the opposing player.

In addition to groundstrokes are **lobs**, volleys, **overheads**, and **drop shots**. A lob is a shot that sails up in the air. Often, a player will lob the ball if his or her opponent is near the net, in which case the ball goes up and over the opponent's head. Or, a player might lob the ball simply to buy time. A volley is a shot made before the ball hits the ground, usually at the net. An overhead, or smash, uses a similar motion to a serve. This is often used to return a lob. Finally, a drop shot is one in which the ball is struck softly, landing just over the net.

athleticism, Venus and Serena—like many other female athletes—have frequently faced sexist comments. Perhaps the most egregious of these came in 2014, when Russian Tennis Federation president Shamil Tarpischev referred to the sisters on a Russian television program as the "Williams brothers." Things went downhill from there, with Tarpischev remarking "It's frightening when you look at them."

Fortunately, the WTA came down hard on Tarpischev. "The statements made by Shamil Tarpischev on Russian television with respect to two of the greatest athletes in the history of women's tennis are insulting, demeaning and have absolutely no place in our sport," said WTA Tour chairman and CEO Stacey Allaster. "Mr. Tarpischev's statements questioning their genders tarnish our great game and two of our champions." The WTA also fined Tarpischev twenty-five thousand dollars—the maximum amount allowed—and banned him for one year.

Serena has faced overt sexism on other occasions as well—particularly with regard to her muscular physique, which some have deemed "unfeminine" or even "manly." (This is particularly ironic because Serena, according to Chris Evert, "is a real girl's girl.") Here's just one example: As noted by journalist Zak Cheney-Rice, the day before Serena was set to compete in the 2015 Wimbledon finals (which she would win), the *New York Times* published an article that did not focus on Serena's status "as one of the most dominant athletes in recent American history." Instead, it talked "at great and invasive length about her body." The now-infamous article claimed that while other players could bulk up like Serena and advance their game, most choose not to. Why? In the case of Agnieszka Radwańska, it was because "she's a woman, and she wants to be a woman." (Incredibly, this statement was made by Radwańska's coach, whose job is to help her improve her tennis skills!)

As Cheney-Rice observed, "One unavoidable takeaway is that Serena Williams' physique must make her less of a woman. Another is that *NYT* page-space the day before the Wimbledon women's final is better spent dissecting the players' bodies than talking about how well they play tennis." Both of these takeaways are undeniably sexist.

Many believe that this type of sexism has had a direct—and negative—impact on Serena's earnings. While she has earned more prize money than any other female player in the history of the game, she has not fared as well as one might expect with endorsements (although she does have deals with Nike, Wilson, Gatorade, Delta Air Lines, Aston Martin, Pepsi, Beats by Dre, Chase Bank, and others). In 2015, Maria Sharapova raked in an astonishing twenty-three million dollars in endorsements. In contrast, Serena pulled just thirteen million dollars. That's still an enormous haul, but why the disparity? After all, as of August 2015, Serena had won 21 majors and spent 247 weeks at number one. In comparison, Sharapova had won just five Grand Slam tournaments and spent only twenty-one weeks at the top spot. Moreover, Serena had dominated in their head-to-head matchups, winning eighteen matches to two. The answer: Many believe it's

A billboard featuring Maria Sharapova.

because Sharapova, who is thin, blonde, and, it must be said, white, more closely mirrors the so-called feminine ideal.

Serena doesn't let the criticism get to her. "It's me, and I love me," she told *Good Morning America*. "I love how I look. I am a full woman and I'm strong, and I'm powerful, and I'm beautiful at the same time." Besides, she added, "I don't have time to be brought down. I've got too many things to do. I have Grand Slams to win, I have people to inspire, and that's what I'm here for." As for the disparity in the endorsements, Serena graciously noted, "There is enough at the table for everyone."

Dealing with Racism

Some believe that racism, too, has played a part in the constant criticism of Serena's body. As noted in the *New Yorker*, "The bodies of athletes, both male and female, are habitually on display, yet there has been something especially contentious and fraught about the ways in which Williams's singular appearance—musculature both imposing and graceful—has been discussed."

Comments of a racist nature are particularly rampant on social media, where Serena has been described as a "gorilla," a "savage," and worse. Why the vitriol? According to Celeste Watkins-Hayes, an associate professor of sociology and African-American studies at Northwestern University, "It's not just that there's a black woman playing in the sport. But it's a black woman playing a sport that's been dominated, when we look at both players and audience, by wealthier whites." Indeed, before Venus and Serena stormed the court, very few African Americans had made it as professional tennis players—in large part due to the game's white-bread past.

Unfortunately, Serena has dealt with comments of a racist nature since childhood. Once, when Serena was just five or six years old, a group of children taunted her and Venus as they practiced on a local court. "They called us Blackie One and Blackie Two," Serena recalled. "It was so cruel, so arbitrary." (How did the girls respond? "We kept playing," Serena said.)

To combat the effects of such comments, Richard Williams took an unorthodox approach: "To toughen the girls' 'skin,'" Richard recalled, "I used to bring busloads of kids from the local schools into Compton to surround the courts while Venus and Serena practiced. I had the kids call them every curse word in the English language"—including the "n-word." Richard added, "I paid them to do it, and I told them to 'do their worst.'"

This training paid off handsomely that day in 2001 at Indian Wells, when Serena and her family were met with racist taunts. "All she had to do was remember the training she had been through," Richard said later. Rather than respond to the attacks, Serena kept her head and focused on her match—which she won. That's not to say it didn't hurt. "She spent the next several hours weeping in the locker room," *Vogue* reported. But it didn't break her, either. Serena took a stand, boycotting the tournament for fourteen years.

Before Indian Wells, Serena took another powerful stand against racism. In 2000, the National Association for the Advancement of Colored People (NAACP) organized a boycott of the state of South Carolina to protest the flying of the Confederate flag over the statehouse. In support of the boycott, Serena pulled out of the Family Circle Cup in Hilton Head. Ultimately, the boycott was successful; the flag was moved elsewhere on the grounds that same year.

"You don't make these stands to accomplish a specific goal," Serena said later. "You make them because they're right. You make them because you wouldn't be here if someone didn't make them for you, long before you were even born." Finally, she added, "You make them because you can, and because you must."

When it comes to combatting racism—and, for that matter, sexism—Serena is up to the challenge. "I play for me," she told the *New York Times* in 2015. "But I also play and represent something much greater than me." She added, "I embrace that. I love that."

CHAPTER SIX

Looking Ahead

During the course of her tennis career, Serena Williams has, quite literally, won everything there is to win. She has collected twenty-one Grand Slam singles titles—a number that grows to thirty-six when you count her thirteen Grand Slam doubles titles and her two mixed doubles titles. When one accounts for all the rest of the tournaments on the women's tour, Serena's stats become even more impressive. As of this writing, she's won an incredible 69 WTA singles titles, with an overall match win-loss record of 737 to 123. And she's reached the number one spot six different times in her career, holding it for a total of 279 weeks as of December 2015.

Serena receives the Sports Illustrated Sportsman of the Year award from her sister Venus.

It's no surprise that Serena has received countless awards. In 1998, she was awarded WTA Newcomer of the Year. The next year, she claimed the WTA Most Improved Player of the Year award. And she's won that organization's Player of the Year award an impressive seven times. Only Steffi Graf has won more (eight). But that's not all. Serena has also won the Associated Press Female Athlete of the Year award on four separate occasions (in 2002, 2009, 2013, and 2015). She has claimed eight ESPY Awards—six for Best Female Tennis Player and two for Best Female Athlete. In 2009, *Sports Illustrated* called Serena the Best Female Athlete of the Decade, and 2015 it named her Sportsperson of the Year—the first time in more than thirty years a woman has won that award on her own. And she has twice been named one of *Time* magazine's 100 Most Influential People, in 2010 and 2014.

Retirement

Serena Williams, thirty-four years old at the time of this writing, shows no signs of slowing down—although her competitors no doubt wish she would! (After Serena defeated close friend Caroline Wozniacki in a recent match, a frustrated Wozniacki wailed, "Will you retire?" Still, at her relatively advanced age—for a professional tennis player, at least—it's only a matter of time before Serena will be forced to hang up her racquet.

When Serena *does* retire, she'll have plenty to keep her busy. Thanks to her parents, who encouraged her and

Venus to be more than just tennis players, Serena is a well-rounded woman with lots of outside interests. As Serena wrote in her autobiography, "When my body tells me it's time to stop chasing and smashing tennis balls for a living, I'll go on and do something else." And, says Serena, "maybe it'll be the something else that helps me leave my true mark. Maybe tennis is just a way for me to get from where I was to where I'm going." Sportswriter Bonnie D. Ford put it this way: "When the sisters do retire, they won't come back. They have plenty to fill the competitive void."

So what are those interests? Serena has expressed a deep interest in fashion. She has also said she'd like to work as an actress. In addition, Serena is interested in philanthropy. And of course, she has her faith and her family to keep her busy.

Fashion

Serena has long been noted for her fashion sense—both on and off the court. As but one example, Serena turned heads at the 2002 US Open by playing in a black Lycra cat suit. "Eccentric. Daring. Adventurous. Fun. Call it whatever you want, but I very quickly developed my own flair," Serena wrote in her autobiography.

But Serena has done more than just *wear* clothes. She has also designed them. "From the very beginning, Puma wanted me to work with them on their designs," she recalled. "By that point, I guess I'd developed a kind of trademark look on the court, so they sought my input."

Soon, Serena took her interest in fashion even further—with a little push from Venus. "I graduated a year early from high school and never really saw the need to continue with my education," Serena explained. Venus, on the other hand, signed up for fashion and design classes at the Art Institute of Fort Lauderdale, which she completed during the off-season. "V was on me all the time to join her at school," Serena recalled. But Serena, who preferred to spend her off-season on the couch watching reruns of *The Golden Girls*, "was too busy doing nothing." Fed up, Venus took charge. She simply signed Serena up for classes. "That's it," Venus said. "I'm tired of watching you waste your time like this. You're going to college."

"Leave it to my big sister to know what was best for me," Serena said. "School was a blast." Like Venus, Serena studied fashion and design. "Most of my courses had me sewing and drawing and learning the construction of a garment, considering which fabric might work on which designs," Serena said. Although Serena did not complete her degree—her tennis schedule was just too arduous—she learned a lot. "I really knew my stuff when I sat down with those Puma designers to develop a new line."

Serena didn't stop there, however. In the years to come, she would launch her own fashion line on the Home Shopping Network (HSN), called Aneres (or "Serena" spelled backward). She would also design her own handbag and jewelry collection, also with HSN, called Serena Williams Signature Statement. In September 2015, Serena revealed a new collection with HSN during New York Fashion Week.

Serena Williams hits the runway to close her fashion show during New York Fashion Week in 2015.

In 2015, Serena also worked with Nike to develop the Serena Greatness collection. In addition to clothing that can be worn on court, the collection featured dresses, shoes, and a bomber-style jacket meant for off-court antics. "It's such a tremendous validation to be in business with people who value your contribution, to know you're not just lending your name to the endeavor but your creativity as well," Serena has said of her various collaborations. (Not to be outdone by her little sister, Venus—who *did* complete her degree in fashion—has launched her own line of action wear, called EleVen by Venus.)

Why this passion for fashion? Serena put it this way: "You're out there as a designer, exposed, vulnerable, and if people respond to your creations there's such a gratifying feeling of accomplishment that comes your way as a result." And, she has said, "I love seeing something on paper and then seeing it in real life."

Hollywood

Shortly after her tennis career achieved liftoff, Serena caught the acting bug. This was no passing fancy, however. Serena even went so far as to hire an acting coach! Since then, Serena has performed in several TV shows and movies. She's even performed in music videos, including one with Common, who Serena was dating at the time. (Other performers in that production included Alicia Keys and Kanye West.) Serena has also appeared in commercials and modeled for magazines, such as the *Sports Illustrated Swimsuit Issue*, *Vogue* (she appeared on the cover in 2015), and others.

Because of her tennis schedule, Serena tends to limit herself to small roles. She has guest-starred on such popular shows as *The Bernie Mac Show*, *ER*, *My Wife and Kids*, *Law & Order: Special Victims Unit*, *Street Time*, *The Division, and Drop Dead Diva*. She has also shared her vocal talents on such animated shows as *The Simpsons*, *Higglytown Heroes*, and *Avatar: The Last Airbender* ("my favorite show," Serena said). In 2015, she appeared in a cameo in the film *Pixels*. In 2005, she and Venus starred in their own reality show, *Venus & Serena: For Real*, which aired on ABC Family. And in 2009, Serena told reporters she was in the process of developing her own TV show—she described it as a cross between *Desperate Housewives*, *Sex and the City*, and *Family Guy*. That project, however, had yet to come to fruition as of December 2015.

Philanthropy

"My parents raised us in a home where giving back was a normal part of life," Serena has said. "As I've gotten older, I've realized how lucky I am to see the difference generosity

Serena Williams: NFL Team Owner

In August 2009, Venus and Serena purchased a small stake in the Miami Dolphins football team, whose stadium is situated about an hour from Serena's home in Palm Beach Gardens, Florida. In doing so, they became the first African-American women to hold an ownership stake in an NFL team. "We're just 'Go Fins!'—type people," Serena said at the time.

Majority owner Stephen Ross made sure the sisters felt welcome, noting, "We are thrilled to have Venus and Serena join the Dolphins as limited partners." Venus and Serena were equally ecstatic. "I am so excited to be part of such a renowned organization," Serena said. "We look forward to many championships and much success together with the Miami Dolphins." The sisters also declared they would attend as many games as possible, schedule permitting.

To commemorate their ownership, Ross presented Venus and Serena with custom-made jerseys. Venus's jersey bore the number eleven, in honor of her fashion line. Serena's featured the number eighty-nine—a nod to their late sister Yetunde, who was born on August 9.

makes in a person's life. It brings me a lot of joy." Thanks to her global platform, Serena has a rare opportunity to assist others—and she regularly does just that through the Serena Williams Foundation. The Serena Williams Foundation has two main areas of focus. One is ensuring that all kids have access to an education. The other is helping those affected by gun violence—a nod to her beloved sister Yetunde.

One of Serena's favorite charities is UNICEF. Serena first teamed up with this important organization in 2006, while on her first visit to Africa. Together, Serena and a team of health workers provided vaccines and medication and distributed free bed nets to help prevent malaria, a devastating disease spread by mosquitos. During that trip, Serena also laid plans to build a free school in Senegal.

Since that time, Serena has become a United Nations Children's Fund (UNICEF) Goodwill Ambassador. In that capacity, Serena works to raise awareness of the organization's mission "to provide a quality education for the most vulnerable children through the Schools for Africa program." And in a partnership with another organization called Build African Schools, Serena has helped to fund the construction of additional free schools in Africa, including the Serena Williams Secondary School in Matooni, Kenya. "Build African Schools is such an incredible foundation," Serena said. "For about $60,000 they can build and outfit an entire schoolhouse, solar-powered and good to go." She added, "What better investment can I make with my money than in the shared futures of these desperately poor Kenyan children?"

Serena visits the Serena Williams Secondary School in Kenya.

Serena's not just concerned with kids in Africa, however. She also works to ensure kids back home have a fair shot. To that end, she has established the Serena Williams Scholars, which offers college scholarships to deserving kids in need. "I'm very passionate about giving back to children," Serena has said. "I think we can all relate to the child in us and what it's like to have big dreams."

To help those affected by violence, Serena has partnered with the Caliber Foundation. Its mission is to support victims, families, and communities affected by illegal gun violence in America. As noted on the charity's website, "The Caliber Foundation offers a helping hand when it is needed, acts of generosity on the parts of many, to help families and communities heal and work together." The organization also melts down illegal guns and casings swept from crime scenes into jewelry, using the proceeds from its sale to fund a gun buyback program. "To date, the Caliber Collection has taken over 1,000 illegal guns off the streets and raised approximately $100,000 for police departments in Newark, Hartford, the San Francisco Bay Area and Detroit from the sales of our products." Interestingly, Serena also supports the Equal Justice Initiative (EJI), which provides legal help to poor defendants and to prisoners who have been denied a fair trial. Serena described EJI as "an amazing organization that has a lot of potential to change lives."

Family

The Williams sisters. Venus and Serena. Serena and Venus. It's almost impossible to talk about one without the other. Perhaps even more than most siblings, Venus and Serena have a shared history—one that only they can understand.

When they were children, Serena hero-worshipped her sister. What Venus had, Serena wanted—always. In her autobiography, Serena tells a story that exemplifies her admiration of her sister about the first time she faced Venus in a tournament.

Venus had earned the right to play the Southern California circuit by beating her father on the court. Serena, on the other hand, was still waiting for her chance. One day, when Serena was just eight years old, she found two blank applications for an upcoming tournament on her father's

Serena's Strong Faith

Serena is a Jehovah's Witness, and her Christian faith is important to her . No doubt, her impulse to give stems in large part from her strong faith. Indeed, according to Serena, faith is "at the root of everything I do, everything I believe. It's what gets me out of bed each morning before first light, to head out to the tennis court. And it's what keeps me believing that anything is possible—not just on the court, but all around."

Although Serena does not speak often in public about her faith, she is known for thanking "Jehovah God" after each match. She has also spoken about spreading the word of God in service of her faith. For Serena, it is her religious faith that has allowed her to push through all of the difficult moments in her life—her injuries, the loss of her sister, Yetunde, and her struggles and losses in her professional career—and to still push ahead onto the next challenge.

As she wrote in her autobiography, "I'm striving, reaching, pushing. Searching. I'm doing my best to please my God, Jehovah, wherever I happen to find Him in my life."

desk. One of them was obviously for Venus. The other one, she claimed for herself. Telling no one, she filled it out and sent it in.

When the family arrived at the tournament, Serena snuck off to play her first match of the day. Incredibly, she won it. And the next one. And the one after that. Suddenly, Serena realized, she was in the finals—against Venus. It would be the first—but far from the last—time the girls faced each other in tournament play. Serena lost, 6-2, 6-2. "I tried my best," Serena said, "but she was playing at a whole other level."

At the awards ceremony, Venus received a gold trophy. Serena's trophy was silver. "I just kept looking at Venus's gold trophy and wishing I could have somehow beaten her," she said. "Oh my God, I wanted that gold trophy so badly." And then Venus, sensing her sister's disappointment, did something Serena would never forget. "You know what, Serena?" Venus said. "I've been thinking. I've always liked silver better than gold. You want to trade?" "To this day," Serena said, that's the most meaningful trophy I've ever received. I didn't earn it, but I cherish it." In fact, she keeps it at her bedside.

This story does more than reveal the sisters' dynamic. It reveals Serena's incredible confidence, given to her—given to both girls—by their parents. "They taught [Venus and Serena] well," observed former pro player Rennae Stubbs of Richard and Oracene. "I think above all they taught them an unbelievable amount of self-esteem and the ability to be champions."

Richard put it this way: "You can make your kids think they are weak or you can make them think they are strong." Clearly, Richard and Oracene made their kids think they were strong. They taught their kids

Serena Williams with her sisters and their mother. From left to right: Lyndrea, Venus, Oracene, Isha, and Serena.

something else, too: "to love themselves so they would have the confidence to make good decisions and strong commitments." While entering a tournament without a parent's permission might not constitute a good decision, it clearly demonstrates strong commitment! This no doubt explains why, rather than being angry at Serena for going against his wishes, Richard simply cheered her on after her secret had been revealed.

Here's another story that reveals much about the sisters' relationship. In 2008, at the US Open, a reporter asked Serena how many Grand Slam titles she might have won had she not faced Venus in the draw. It was a fair question—after all, Venus had knocked Serena out of five different Grand Slam tournaments. No doubt, the reporter believed Serena could have won many more majors without Venus in the way. But Serena saw things differently. "I don't think I would have won nearly as many," she said. Serena told the reporter "how growing up in Venus's shadow has been such a powerful motivator for me. How the impossible standard she set on the court (and off!) was such a powerful model. How she pushed me to be the very best that I could be."

Venus and Serena have always been close, and it's likely they always will be. Even today, the sisters share a mansion in Florida—something they've done since they were both in their teens. Richard, who remarried in 2011 and once again became a father the next year, lives just fifteen minutes away and visits often. Venus and Serena speak almost daily to their mother, who lives in Los Angeles, and to their remaining sisters. For the Williams sisters, it's clear that family is everything.

And what of starting her own family? Although Serena has been in several relationships over the years, she has yet to find Mr. Right. Indeed, relationships have been so frustrating for Serena that she declared in 2012 that she had "given up dating." She explained, "It just hasn't worked out for me." Still, she has said that she would like to have children. In 2014, during a question and answer session on Twitter, a fan asked if she wanted to settle down and have kids. Serena responded, "Desperately." She added, "My time will come." Another fan asked if she was single. Her reply: "Not by choice."

Whatever she decides to do next—start a new career, become a mother, or something else entirely—one thing is clear: Serena Williams will do it beautifully.

Timeline

1995

Serena plays in her first pro tournament in October but loses in the first round to Anne Miller.

1999

Serena's breakout year. She wins five tournaments, including the US Open, and ends the year ranked number four in the world.

2001

Serena wins at Indian Wells in front of an extremely hostile crowd. She boycotts the tournament for the next fourteen years.

1981

Serena Williams is born on September 26 to Richard and Oracene Williams.

The Williams family moves to Florida so Serena and her sister Venus can receive additional tennis instruction.

1991

Serena enjoys her first taste of success at the Ameritech Cup Chicago in November, where she advances as far as the semifinals, beating world number seven Mary Pierce and world number four Monica Seles en route.

1997

Richard Williams watches Virginia Ruzici win the final of a women's tennis tournament and claim a cash prize of forty thousand dollars. This inspires him to have two daughters and teach them to play tennis.

1978

2003

Serena injures her knee in July and is sidelined from tennis for several months. On September 14, Serena's beloved half-sister Yetunde is murdered in Compton, California.

2010

Following a severe foot injury, Serena is sidelined for several months and her rating drops to 169.

2015

In March, Serena returns to Indian Wells for the first time since 2001. In July, Serena wins Wimbledon to complete her second Serena Slam and her twenty-first Grand Slam title.

2008

Serena reclaims the number one spot in the rankings.

2012

Serena claims gold in women's singles at the London Olympics in August, completing a career Golden Slam.

Serena completes her first "Serena Slam," claiming the French Open, Wimbledon, the US Open, and the Australian Open in succession. In July, she claims the world number one ranking for the first time in her career.

An overweight, out-of-shape Serena stuns the world by winning the Australian Open title in January.

2007

Once again, Serena reclaims the number one spot—a position she still holds at the time of this writing.

2002

Serena, having fallen to 139 in the rankings, begins her comeback. She also visits Africa for the first time—a life-changing trip.

2013

2006

SOURCE NOTES

Chapter One

Page 5: Williams, Serena, and Daniel Paisner. *On the Line* (New York: Grand Central Publishing, 2009), p. 11.

Page 6: "Tennis; Status: Undefeated. Future: Rosy. Age 10" www.nytimes.com/1990/07/03/sports/tennis-status-undefeated-future-rosy-age-10.html.

Page 6: Williams, Richard, and Bart Davis. *Black and White: The Way I See It* (New York: Atria Books, 2014), p. 162.

Page 7: Williams and Paisner, *On the Line*, p. 46.

Page 8: Williams and Davis, *Black and White: The Way I See It*, p. 163.

Page 8: Williams and Davis, *Black and White: The Way I See It*, p. 20.

Page 8: Williams and Davis, *Black and White: The Way I See It*, p. 21.

Page 8: Williams and Davis, *Black and White: The Way I See It*, p. 55.

Page 10: Williams and Davis, *Black and White: The Way I See It*, p. 190.

Page 10: Williams and Paisner, *On the Line*, p. 13.

Page 10: Williams and Davis, *Black and White: The Way I See It*, p. 196.

Page 10: Williams and Davis, *Black and White: The Way I See It*, p. 197.

Page10: Williams and Davis, *Black and White: The Way I See It*, p. 207.

Page 11: Hsu, Huan. "Wanted: Insane Tennis Parents." www.slate.com/articles/sports/sports_nut/2009/06/wanted_insane_tennis_parents.html.

Page 11: Cobello, Dominic, Mike Agassi, and Kate Shoup Welsh. *The Agassi Story*. (Toronto, Canada: ECW Press, 2004), p. 81.

Page 11: Hsu, "Wanted: Insane Tennis Parents."

Page 12: Martin, Douglas. "Peter Graf, Volatile Father of Tennis Great, Dies at 75," www.nytimes.com/2013/12/04/sports/peter-graf-volatile-father-of-tennis-great-dies-at-75.html.

Page 12: Williams and Davis, *Black and White: The Way I See It*, p. 261.

Page 12: Williams and Paisner, *On the Line*, p. 13.

Page 13: Williams and Paisner, *On the Line*, p. 105.

Page 13: Williams and Davis, *Black and White: The Way I See It*, p. 213.

Page 13: Sullivan, John Jeremiah. "Venus and Serena Against the World," www.nytimes.com/2012/08/26/magazine/venus-and-serena-against-the-world.htm.

Page13: Sullivan, "Venus and Serena Against the World."

Page 13: Sullivan, "Venus and Serena Against the World."

Page 14: Williams and Paisner, *On the Line*, p. 9.

Page 14: Williams and Davis, *Black and White: The Way I See It*, p. 210.

Page 14: Williams and Paisner, *On the Line*, p. 19.

Page 14: Williams and Davis, *Black and White: The Way I See It*, p. 210.

Page 15: Peebles, Maurice. "Serena Williams' Childhood Coach: 'She Will Be No. 1 in the World, Or She Will Go to Jail,'"www.complex.com/sports/2015/09/rick-macci-interview.

Page 15: Ford, Bonnie D. "Williams sisters' parents deserve accolades for job well-done," sports.espn.go.com/sports/tennis/usopen08/columns/story?columnist=ford_bonnie_d&id=3556008.

Page 15: Williams and Paisner, *On the Line,* p. 88.

Page 15: Wiedeman, Reeves. "Child's Play," http://www.newyorker.com/magazine/2014/06/02/childs-play-6 .

Page 15: Williams and Davis, *Black and White: The Way I See It,* p. 212.

Chapter Two

Page 17: Sullivan, "Venus and Serena Against the World."

Page18: Williams and Paisner, *On the Line*, p. 48.

Page 18: Williams and Paisner, *On the Line*, p. 46.

Page 18: Williams and Paisner, *On the Line*, p. 115.

Page 18: Sullivan, "Venus and Serena Against the World."

Page 18: "Tennis; Status: Undefeated. Future: Rosy. Age 10."

Page 18: "Tennis; Status: Undefeated. Future: Rosy. Age 10."

Page 18: Williams and Paisner, *On the Line*, p. 44.

Page 19: Williams and Paisner, *On the Line*, p. 43.

Page 19: Walker, Randy. "Rick Macci on His First Meeting Richard, Venus and Serena Williams," www.tennisgrandstand.com/2014/04/22/rick-macci-on-his-first-meeting-richard-venus-and-serena-williams.

Page 19: Walker, Randy. "Rick Macci on His First Meeting Richard, Venus and Serena Williams."

Page 20: Walker, Randy. "Rick Macci on His First Meeting Richard, Venus and Serena Williams."

Page 20: Williams and Paisner, *On the Line*, p. 95.

Page 20: Williams and Paisner, *On the Line*, p. 94.

Page 21: Williams and Paisner, *On the Line*, p. 92.

Page 21: Williams and Paisner, *On the Line*, p. 102.

Page 22: Peebles, Maurice. "Serena Williams' Childhood Coach: 'She Will Be No. 1 in the World, Or She Will Go to Jail.'"

Page 23: Williams and Paisner, *On the Line*, p. 100.

Page 23: Williams and Davis, *Black and White: The Way I See It*, p. 187.

Page 23: Williams and Paisner, *On the Line*, p. 103.

Page 23: Sullivan, "Venus and Serena Against the World."

Page 24: Williams and Paisner, *On the Line*, p. 103-104.

Page 25: Williams and Paisner, *On the Line*, p. 111.

Page 25: Williams and Paisner, *On the Line*, p. 112.

Page 25: Williams and Paisner, *On the Line*, p. 113.

Page 26: Williams and Paisner, *On the Line*, p. 112.

Page 26: Isaacson, Melissa. "Whatever Happened to the First Person to Beat Serena Williams?" espn.go.com/espnw/news-commentary/article/12167370/what-ever-happened-first-person-beat-serena-williams.

Page 26: Isaacson, Melissa. "Whatever Happened to the First Person to Beat Serena Williams?"

Page 28: Williams and Paisner, *On the Line*, p. 115.

Page 31: Price, S. L. "Who's Your Daddy?"

Chapter Three

Page 33–34: Williams and Davis, *Black and White: The Way I See It*, pp. 242–243.

Page 34: Williams and Paisner, *On the Line*, pp. 120-121.

Page 36: Williams and Davis, *Black and White: The Way I See It*, p. 251.

Page 36: Williams and Paisner, *On the Line*, p. 64.

Page 36: Williams and Davis, *Black and White: The Way I See It*, p. 251.

Page 36: Williams and Paisner, *On the Line*, p. 67.

Page 37: Williams and Davis, *Black and White: The Way I See It*, p. 252.

Page 37: Williams and Paisner, *On the Line*, p. 57.

Page 37: Williams and Paisner, *On the Line*, p. 70.

Page 37: Williams and Davis, *Black and White: The Way I See It*, p. 255.

Page 37: Williams and Paisner, *On the Line*, p. 71.

Page 38: Williams and Paisner, *On the Line*, p. 80.

Page 38: Williams and Davis, *Black and White: The Way I See It*, p. 257.

Page 39: Williams and Davis, *Black and White: The Way I See It*, p. 252.

Page 39: Williams and Paisner, *On the Line*, p. 76.

Page 39: Williams, Serena. "Serena Williams: I'm Going Back to Indian Wells," time.com/3694659/serena-williams-indian-wells.

Page 39: Rothenberg, Ben. "This Time, Serena Williams Is Cheered as She Leaves Indian Wells," www.nytimes.com/2015/03/22/sports/tennis/this-time-serena-williams-is-cheered-as-she-leaves-indian-wells.html

Page 39: Williams and Paisner, *On the Line*, p. 138.

Page 39: Williams and Paisner, *On the Line*, p. 143.

Page 39–40: *Ibid.*

Page 41: *Ibid.*

Page 42: Williams and Paisner, *On the Line*, p. 146.

Page 43–44: Williams and Paisner, *On the Line*, p. 147.

Page 44: Pierson, David, and Richard Fausset. "Family Came First for Slain Sibling," http://articles.latimes.com/2003/sep/25/local/me-price25.

Page 45: Williams and Davis, *Black and White: The Way I See It*, p. 278.

Chapter Four

Page 47: Williams and Paisner, *On the Line,* p. 165.

Page 47–48: Williams and Paisner, *On the Line,* p. 167.

Page 48: Williams and Paisner, *On the Line,* p. 172.

Page 48: Williams and Paisner, *On the Line,* p. 173.

Page 48: Williams and Paisner, *On the Line,* pp. 174–175.

Page 49: Williams and Paisner, *On the Line,* p.198.

Page 49: Williams and Paisner, *On the Line,* p. 199.

Page 50: Williams and Paisner, *On the Line,* p. 197.

Page 50: Williams and Paisner, *On the Line,* p. 199.

Page 50–51: Williams and Paisner, *On the Line,* pp. 201–202.

Page 52: Williams and Paisner, *On the Line,* p. 180.

Page 52: Williams and Paisner, *On the Line,* p. 184.

Page 52: Williams and Paisner, *On the Line,* p. 183.

Page 52-53: Williams and Paisner, *On the Line,* p. 184.

Page 53: Williams and Paisner, *On the Line,* p. 185.

Page 53: Williams and Paisner, *On the Line,* p. 202.

Page 53: Williams and Paisner, *On the Line,* p. 204.

Page 53: Williams and Paisner, *On the Line,* p. 205.

Page 53: Williams and Paisner, *On the Line,* p. 185.

Page 54: Williams and Paisner, *On the Line,* pp. 208–209.

Page 55: Williams and Paisner, *On the Line,* p. 210.

Page 55: Williams and Paisner, *On the Line,* p. 213.

Page 55: Williams and Paisner, *On the Line,* p. 225.

Page 55: Williams and Paisner, *On the Line*, p. 228.

Page 57: Crouse, Karen. "Williams Sisters Write Their Own Story." www.nytimes.com/2009/08/31/sports/tennis/31williams.html.

Page 58: Cherner, Reid. "Tennis Star Serena Williams Home After Treatment for Blood Clot," content.usatoday.com/communities/gameon/post/2011/03/serena-williams-has-emergency-health-treatement.

Chapter Five

Page 62: Zagoria, Adam. "Chris Evert, Billie Jean King Call Serena Williams Greatest Ever," www.metro.us/sports/legends-evert-king-call-serena-williams-greatest-ever-metro-us.

Page 62: Rankine, Claudia. "The Meaning of Serena Williams," www.nytimes.com/2015/08/30/magazine/the-meaning-of-serena-williams.html.

Page 62: Corpuz, Rachelle. "Andre Agassi Says Serena Williams Is The 'Greatest Ever'." www.ibtimes.com.au/andre-agassi-says-serena-williams-greatest-ever-1426225.

Page 62: Rankine, Claudia. "The Meaning of Serena Williams."

Page 63: Crouch, Ian. "Serena Williams Is America's Greatest Athlete," www.newyorker.com/news/sporting-scene/serena-williams-americas-greatest-athlete.

Page 63: Schiavenza, Matt. "The Astonishing Greatness of Serena Williams," www.theatlantic.com/entertainment/archive/2015/07/the-astonishing-greatness-of-serena-williams/398339.

Page 63: *Ibid.*

Page 63: Johnson, Rebecca. "Why Serena Williams Is Best Friends with Her Fiercest Competitor." www.vogue.com/12135713/serena-williams-april-cover-caroline-wozniacki.

Page 63: Schiavenza, Matt. "The Astonishing Greatness of Serena Williams."

Page 64: Allen, J.A. "The Williams Sisters and the Rise of the Power Game," bleacherreport.com/articles/1350759-the-williams-sisters-and-the-rise-of-the-womens-power-game.

Page 64: Crouse, Karen. "Williams Sisters Write Their Own Story."

Page 64: "Girl Power: Evolution of the Women's Game." www.tennis-head.net/news/on-tour/2011/12/15/girl-power-evolution-of-the-womens-game

Page 65: Kimmelman, Michael. "How Power Has Transformed Women's Tennis," www.nytimes.com/2010/08/29/magazine/29Tennis-t.html

Page 65: "Girl Power: Evolution of the Women's Game."

Page 66: Allen, J.A. "The Williams Sisters and the Rise of the Power Game."

pg. 67: Williams and Davis, *Black and White: The Way I See It,* pp. 240-241.

Page 67: "Shamil Tarpischev Fined, Banned Year,". espn.go.com/tennis/story/_/id/11718876/russian-tennis-federation-president-shamil-tarpischev-sanctioned-serena-venus-williams-gender-comments.

Page 67: "Shamil Tarpischev Fined, Banned Year."

Page 68 Johnson, Rebecca. "Why Serena Williams Is Best Friends with Her Fiercest Competitor."

Page 68: Cheney-Rice, Zak. "Serena Williams Just Won Her 21st Major. So Why Are We Still Talking About Her Body?" mic.com/articles/122186/serena-williams-just-won-her-21st-major-so-why-are-we-still-talking-about-her-body.

Page 68: *Ibid.*

Page 69: Maine, D'Arcy. "Serena Williams Shades Body Shamers: 'I've Got Grand Slams to Win'," espn.go.com/espnw/athletes-life/the-buzz/article/13550586/got-grand-slams-win.

Page 69: Rankine, Claudia. "The Meaning of Serena Williams."

Page 70: Crouch, Ian. "Serena Williams Is America's Greatest Athlete."

Page 70: Snyder, Deron. "Regardless of Appearance, Serena Williams a Champion Who Can't Win," www.washingtontimes.com/news/2015/jul/15/serena-williams-appearance-proud-muscular-toned/?page=all.

Page 70: Williams and Paisner, *On the Line,* p. 15.

Page 71: Williams and Davis, *Black and White: The Way I See It*, p. 229.

Page 71: Riddell, Don, and Gary Morley. "U.S. Open 2015: Serena Williams' Father 'Not Surprised' by James Blake Arrest." edition.cnn.com/2015/09/11/tennis/richard-williams-serena-venus-tennis.

Page 71: Johnson, Rebecca. "Why Serena Williams Is Best Friends with Her Fiercest Competitor."

Page 71: Williams and Paisner, *On the Line*, p. 15.

Page71: Rankine, Claudia. "The Meaning of Serena Williams."

Chapter Six

pg. 74: Johnson, Rebecca. "Why Serena Williams Is Best Friends with Her Fiercest Competitor."

pg. 75: Williams and Paisner, *On the Line*, p. 257.

Page 75: Williams and Paisner, *On the Line*, p. 130.

Page 76: Williams and Paisner, *On the Line,* p. 131.

Page 76: Williams and Paisner, *On the Line*, p. 132.

Page 77: Williams and Paisner, *On the Line*, pp. 133–134.

Page 77: *Ibid.*

Page 78: Yotka, Steff. "Why You Should Be Paying Attention to Serena Williams's Fashion Collection," www.vogue.com/13337317/serena-williams-hsn-collection-drake.

Page 78: Kennedy, Lauren Paige. "Serena Williams Gets Back in the Game," www.webmd.com/women/features/serena-williams-gets-back-game.

Page 79: Associated Press. "Williams Sisters Buy into Dolphins Group." espn.go.com/nfl/news/story?id=4422313.

Page 79: Marx, Linda. "Williams Sisters Buy Stake in Miami Dolphins," www.people.com/people/article/0,,20300197,00.html.

Page 80: Elliott, Danielle. "Serena Williams: A Powerful Serve, and a Powerful Commitment to Service." www.chase.com/news/081315-serena-williams.

Page 80: "Serena Williams Fund," serenawilliams.com/swfund.

Page 81: Williams and Paisner, *On the Line*, p. 192.

Page 81: Elliott, Danielle. "Serena Williams: A Powerful Serve, and a Powerful Commitment to Service."

Page 82: "The Caliber Collection: Who We Are," www.calibercollection.com/?page_id=4602.

Page 82: Elliott, Danielle. "Serena Williams: A Powerful Serve, and a Powerful Commitment to Service."

Page 83: Williams and Paisner, *On the Line*, p. 86.

Page 83: Williams and Paisner, *On the Line*, p. 89.

Page 84: Williams and Paisner, *On the Line*, pp. 53-54.

Page 84: *Ibid.*

Page 85: Ford, Bonnie D. "Williams sisters' parents deserve accolades for job well-done."

Page 85: Williams and Davis, *Black and White: The Way I See It*, p. 159.

Page 85: Williams and Davis, *Black and White: The Way I See It*, p. 35.

Page 86: Williams and Paisner, *On the Line*, p. 59.

Page 87: "Heartbroken Serena Williams: I Don't Want to Date for the Next Decade." www.celebuzz.com/2012-05-01/heartbroken-serena-williams-i-dont-want-to-date-for-the-next-decade-exclusive.

Page 87: Chase, Chris. "Serena Williams Says She 'Desperately' Wants to Have Children." ftw.usatoday.com/2014/11/serena-williams-serenafriday-twitter-children.

GLOSSARY

backhand A type of shot in tennis in which the player swings the racquet across his or her body, with the back of the hand preceding the palm. The backhand is a type of groundstroke.

career Grand Slam The act of winning all four Grand Slam tournaments during the course of one's career.

drop shot A type of shot in tennis in which the ball is struck softly, landing just over the net.

forehand A typical tennis shot in which the player swings the racquet along the side of his or her body palm first. The forehand is a type of groundstroke.

game (in tennis scoring) A component of a tennis set. To win a set, a player must win a minimum of six games. However, the player must win by at least two games.

Grand Slam tournament One of the more prestigious events on the tennis circuit; also called a major. There are four Grand Slam tournaments: the Australian Open, the French Open, Wimbledon, and the US Open.

groundstroke A type of tennis shot that bounces off the ground before being struck by the opposing player. Examples of groundstrokes are the forehand and backhand.

lob A type of shot in tennis that sails up in the air. Often, a player will lob the ball if his or her opponent is near the net, in which case the ball goes up and over the opponent's head. Or, a player might lob the ball simply to buy time.

love (in tennis scoring) A score of zero. At the beginning of each game, each player starts at love. Points then progress to 15, 30, 40, and then game (that is, the game is won).

Open Era An era in tennis in which professionals and amateurs alike were permitted to play in Grand Slam and other prestigious tournaments in the hopes of earning prize money. The Open Era began in 1968 and continues to this day.

overhead Also called a smash, a type of shot in tennis that uses a similar motion to a serve. An overhead is often used to return a lob.

purse A sum of money offered as a prize.

seed An athlete in a tournament who has been assigned a number that reflects the likelihood that he or she will win the tournament. The top seed in a tournament is the athlete most likely to win.

serve The shot in tennis that puts the point into play. When serving, the player stands at the baseline, tosses the ball into the air, and brings the racquet up overhead to make contact with the ball.

set A component of a tennis match. To win a match, a player must win a prescribed number of sets. Typically, the number of sets the player must win is three out of five (men) or two out of three (women).

vitriol Virulence, or extreme bitterness, of feeling or of speech.

volley A type of shot in tennis that is made before the ball hits the ground, usually at the net.

FURTHER INFORMATION

Books

Williams, Richard and Bart Davis. *Black and White: The Way I See It*. New York: Atria Books, 2014.

Williams, Serena and Daniel Paisner. *On the Line*. New York: Grand Central Publishing, 2009.

Williams, Venus, Serena Williams, and Hilary Beard. *Venus and Serena: Serving from the Hip: 10 Rules for Living, Loving, and Winning*. New York: HMH Books for Young Readers, 2005.

Websites

Serena Williams's Website

serenawilliams.com

This site includes a blog, Serena's tennis schedule, and clips about her life.

Serena on Facebook

www.facebook.com/SerenaWilliams

Follow Serena's Facebook feed here for updates on her professional schedule and recent charity work.

Serena on Twitter

twitter.com/SerenaWilliams

Serena uses Twitter to keep in touch with fans and holds a question and answer session for fans on Fridays.

Serena on Instagram

www.instagram.com/serenawilliams/?hl=en

Instagram fans can follow Serena here.

Serena Williams at ESPN

espn.go.com/tennis/player/_/id/394/serena-williams

Your online source for Serena stats, news, pictures, video, and more.

Video

Serena Williams Accepts 2015 Sportsperson of the Year Award

www.youtube.com/watch?v=I9eoPS1Rzug

Be inspired by watching Serena accept her 2015 *Sports Illustrated* Sportsperson of the Year Award.

BIBLIOGRAPHY

Allen, J.A. "The Williams Sisters and the Rise of the Women's Power Game." *The Bleacher Report*, September 28, 2012. Accessed February 2, 2016. bleacherreport.com/articles/1350759-the-williams-sisters-and-the-rise-of-the-womens-power-game.

Associated Press. "Williams Sisters Buy into Dolphins Group." ESPN. com, August 25, 2009. Accessed February 4, 2016. espn.go.com/nfl/news/story?id=4422313.

Chase, Chris. "Serena Williams Says She 'Desperately' Wants Children in Twitter Q&A." *USA Today*, November 7, 2014. Accessed February 4, 2016. ftw.usatoday.com/2014/11/serena-williams-serenafriday-twitter-children.

Cheney-Rice, Zak. "Serena Williams Just Won Her 21st Major. So Why Are We Still Talking About Her Body?" mic.com. July 13, 2015. Accessed February 2, 2016. mic.com/articles/122186/serena-williams-just-won-her-21st-major-so-why-are-we-still-talking-about-her-body.

Cherner, Reid. "Tennis Star Serena Williams Home After Treatment for Blood Clot." *USA Today*, March 2, 2011. content.usatoday.com/communities/gameon/post/2011/03/serena-williams-has-emergency-health-treatement.

Cobello, Dominic, Mike Agassi, and Kate Shoup Welsh. *The Agassi Story*. Toronto, Canada: ECW Press, 2004.

Coffey, Wayne. "Court of Last Resort. Former Phenom Hits Back at IMG, Father in Struggle to Return to Top of Tennis World." *New York Daily News*, May 7, 2006. www.nydailynews.com/archives/sports/court-resort-phenom-hits-back-img-father-struggle-return-top-tennis-world-article.

lle. "Andre Agassi Says Serena Williams Is The 'Greatest *ernational Business Times*, March 3, 2015. Accessed February 1, 2016. www.ibtimes.com.au/andre-agassi-says-serena-williams-greatest-ever-1426225.

Crouch, Ian. "Serena Williams Is America's Greatest Athlete." *New Yorker*, September 9, 2014. www.newyorker.com/news/sporting-scene/serena-williams-americas-greatest-athlete.

Crouse, Karen. "Williams Sisters Write Their Own Story." *New York Times*, August 30, 2009. www.nytimes.com/2009/08/31/sports/tennis/31williams.html.

Elliott, Danielle. *Serena Williams: A Powerful Serve, and a Powerful Commitment to Service.* Chase.com, August 12, 2015. Accessed February 4, 2016. www.chase.com/news/081315-serena-williams.

Ford, Bonnie D. "Williams sisters' parents deserve accolades for job well-done." ESPN.com, August 28, 2008. Accessed January 27, 2016. sports.espn.go.com/sports/tennis/usopen08/columns/story?-columnist=ford_bonnie_d&id=3556008.

"Heartbroken Serena Williams: I Don't Want to Date for the Next Decade." Celebuzz.com, May 12, 2012. Accessed February 4, 2016. www.celebuzz.com/2012-05-01/heartbroken-serena-williams-i-dont-want-to-date-for-the-next-decade-exclusive.

Hsu, Huan. "Wanted: Insane Tennis Parents." *Slate*, June 2, 2009. Accessed January 27, 2016. www.slate.com/articles/sports/sports_nut/2009/06/wanted_insane_tennis_parents.html.

Isaacson, Melissa. "Whatever Happened to the First Person to Beat Serena Williams?" ESPN.com, January 15, 2015. Accessed January 28, 2016. espn.go.com/espnw/news-commentary/article/12167370/what-ever-happened-first-person-beat-serena-williams.

Johnson, Rebecca. "Why Serena Williams Is Best Friends with Her Fiercest Competitor." *Vogue*, March 21, 2015. www.vogue.com/12135713/serena-williams-april-cover-caroline-wozniacki.

Kennedy, Lauren Paige. "Serena Williams Gets Back in the Game." *WebMD*. Accessed February 4, 2016. www.webmd.com/women/features/serena-williams-gets-back-game.

Kimmelman, Michael. "How Power Has Transformed Women's Tennis." *New York Times*, August 25, 2010. www.nytimes.com/2010/08/29/magazine/29Tennis-t.html.

Maine, D'Arcy. "Serena Williams Shades Body Shamers: 'I've Got Grand Slams to Win'." ESPN.com, August 31, 2015. Accessed February 2, 2016. espn.go.com/espnw/athletes-life/the-buzz/article/13550586/got-grand-slams-win?ex_cid=espnTW.

Martin, Douglas. "Peter Graf, Volatile Father of Tennis Great, Dies at 75." *New York Times*, December 3, 2013. www.nytimes.com/2013/12/04/sports/peter-graf-volatile-father-of-tennis-great-dies-at-75.html

Marx, Linda. "Williams Sisters Buy Stake in Miami Dolphins." *People*, August 25, 2009. www.people.com/people/article/0,,20300197,00.html.

Merron, Jeff. ESPN.com, n.d. *The List: Sports' Most Harmful Relatives.* Accessed January 28, 2016. espn.go.com/page2/s/list/badblood.html.

Oswald, Kent. "Siblings School: Williams Sisters and Brothers Build Bridge to Better Life." *Tennis Week*, March 6, 2008. http://www.ontennis.com/news/siblings-school-williams-sisters-and-brothers-build-bridge-better-life.

Peebles, Maurice. "Serena Williams' Childhood Coach: 'She Will Be No. 1 in the World, Or She Will Go to Jail.'" *Complex*, September 23, 2015. Accessed January 27, 2016. www.complex.com/sports/2015/09/rick-macci-interview.

Pierson, David, and Richard Fausset. "Family Came First for Slain Sibling." *LA Times*, September 25, 2003. articles.latimes.com/2003/sep/25/local/me-price25.

Price, S. L. "Who's Your Daddy?" *Sports Illustrated*, May 31, 1999. www.si.com/vault/1999/05/31/8107824/whos-your-daddy-call-richard-williams-what-you-wantbizarre-deceitful-or-perhaps-madbut-be-sure-of-one-thing-he-has-brilliantly-guided-the-careers-and-lives-of-his-daughters-venus-and-serena-the-hottest-players-in-tennis.

Rankine, Claudia. "The Meaning of Serena Williams." *New York Times*, August 25, 2015. www.nytimes.com/2015/08/30/magazine/the-meaning-of-serena-williams.html.

Riddell, Don, and Gary Morley. "US Open 2015: Serena Williams' Father 'Not Surprised' by James Blake Arrest." *CNN*, September 11, 2015. Accessed February 2, 2016. edition.cnn.com/2015/09/11/tennis/richard-williams-serena-venus-tennis.

Rothenberg, Ben. "Tennis's Top Women Balance Body Image With Ambition." *New York Times*, July 10, 2015. www.nytimes.com/2015/07/11/sports/tennis/tenniss-top-women-balance-body-image-with-quest-for-success.html.

Rothenberg, Ben. "This Time, Serena Williams Is Cheered as She Leaves Indian Wells." *New York Times*, March 21, 2015. www.nytimes.com/2015/03/22/sports/tennis/this-time-serena-williams-is-cheered-as-she-leaves-indian-wells.html.

Ryan, Shannon. "Why Are Serena Williams' Curves Discussed More Than Her Serves?" *Chicago Tribune*, September 7, 2015. www.chicagotribune.com/sports/ct-smack-serena-williams-ryan-spt-0907-20150906-story.html.

Schiavenza, Matt. "The Astonishing Greatness of Serena Williams." *The Atlantic*, July 11, 2015. www.theatlantic.com/entertainment/archive/2015/07/the-astonishing-greatness-of-serena-williams/398339.

"Serena Williams Fund." Accessed February 4, 2016. serenawilliams.com/swfund.

"Shamil Tarpischev Fined, Banned Year." ESPN.com, October 18, 2014. Accessed February 2, 2016. espn.go.com/tennis/story/_/id/11718876/russian-tennis-federation-president-shamil-tarpischev-sanctioned-serena-venus-williams-gender-comments.

Snyder, Deron. "Regardless of Appearance, Serena Williams a Champion Who Can't Win." *Washington Times*. July 15, 2015. www.washingtontimes.com/news/2015/jul/15/serena-williams-appearance-proud-muscular-toned.

Sullivan, John Jeremiah. "Venus and Serena Against the World." *New York Times Magazine*, August 23, 2012. www.nytimes.com/2012/08/26/magazine/venus-and-serena-against-the-world.html.

"Tennis; Status: Undefeated. Future: Rosy. Age 10." *New York Times*, July 3, 1990. www.nytimes.com/1990/07/03/sports/tennis-status-undefeated-future-rosy-age-10.html.

tennishead. "Girl Power: Evolution of the Women's Game." November, 2011. www.tennishead.net/news/on-tour/2011/12/15/girl-power-evolution-of-the-womens-game.

"The Caliber Collection: Who We Are." Accessed February 4, 2016. www.calibercollection.com/?page_id=4602.

Walker, Randy. *Rick Macci on His First Meeting Richard, Venus and Serena Williams*. April 22, 2014. Accessed February 5, 2016. www.tennisgrandstand.com/2014/04/22/rick-macci-on-his-first-meeting-richard-venus-and-serena-williams.

Wiedeman, Reeves. "Child's Play." *The New Yorker*, June 2, 2014. www.newyorker.com/magazine/2014/06/02/childs-play-6.

Williams, Richard, and Bart Davis. *Black and White: The Way I See It*. New York: Atria Books, 2014.

Williams, Serena. "Serena Williams: I'm Going Back to Indian Wells." *Time*, February 4, 2015. time.com/3694659/serena-williams-indian-wells.

Williams, Serena, and Daniel Paisner. *On the Line*. New York: Grand Central Publishing, 2009.

Williams, Venus. "Our Story." Eleven by Venus Williams. Accessed February 4, 2016. elevenbyvenuswilliams.com/pages/we-are-eleven.

Yotka, Steff. "Why You Should Be Paying Attention to Serena Williams's Fashion Collection." *Vogue*, September 16, 2015. www.vogue.com/13337317/serena-williams-hsn-collection-drake.

Zagoria, Adam. "Chris Evert, Billie Jean King Call Serena Williams Greatest Ever." September 5, 2013. Accessed February 1, 2016. www.metro.us/sports/legends-evert-king-call-serena-williams-greatest-ever-metro-us.

INDEX

Page numbers in **boldface** are illustrations. Entries in **boldface** are glossary terms.

ABOUT THE AUTHOR

Kate Shoup has authored more than thirty books on a variety of topics and has edited scores more. For Cavendish Square, Kate's titles include *Kate Middleton*, *Billie Jean King*, *Texas and the Mexican War*, *The California Gold Rush*, *Life as a Soldier in the Civil War*, *Life as an Engineer on the First Railroads of America*, *Life as a Prospector in the California Gold Rush*, *Egypt*, *India*, *Greece*, and *Rohypnol*. Kate has also co-written a feature-length screenplay (and starred in the ensuing film) and worked as the Sports Editor for *NUVO Newsweekly*. When not writing, Kate, an IndyCar fanatic, loves to ski, read, and ride her motorcycle. She lives in Indianapolis with her husband, her daughter, and their dog.